Life in
THE CASTLE
IN MEDIEVAL ENGLAND

Life in

THE CASTLE IN MEDIEVAL ENGLAND

JOHN BURKE

BRITISH HERITAGE PRESS
New York

This 1983 edition is published by British Heritage Press,
distributed by Crown Publishers, Inc.

Printed in Hong Kong

Library of Congress Cataloging in Publication Data

Burke, John Frederick, 1922–
    Life in the castle in medieval England.

    Reprint. Originally published: London: B. T. Batsford, 1978.
    Bibliography: p.
    Includes index.
    1. Castles—England.   2. England—Social life and
customs—Medieval period, 1066–1485.   I. Title.
II. Title: The castle in medieval England.
DA660.B89   1982   942   82–22690
ISBN 0–517–40511–3

h g f e d c b

Contents

Acknowledgements

The Author and Publisher would particularly like to thank Marian Berman for her picture research and the following for the illustrations which appear in this book:

Aerofilms for figs 5, 54, 60(a) & (b), 63(b); Bibliothèque Nationale, Paris and Weidenfeld & Nicolson fig. 68; Bibliothèque Nationale, Paris figs 28 & 52; Bodleian Library, Oxford figs 42(a), 44, 70; British Library Board figs 1, 2, 14, 15, 17, 23, 24, 25(a), (b) & (c), 27, 31(b), 33(a), (b) & (c), 34, 36, 37, 38, 41, 42(c), 43, 45, 46, 56, 59, 71, 73(b), (c) & (d), 74, 75, 76(a) & (b), 77; Trustees of the British Museum figs 26(b), 32(a), (b) & (c), 48; Master and Fellows of Corpus Christi College, Cambridge figs 51 & 73(a); Country Life fig. 83; Department of the Environment figs 6, 7, 10, 12, 22, 61, 64, 65, 80; Director of Aerial Photography, University of Cambridge fig. 4(a); Durham Cathedral Library fig. 39; A. F. Kersting figs 8, 9, 11, 13, 16, 19, 25(d), 35, 49, 63(a), 67, 79, 84, 85, 87, 88; Museum of London figs 26(a), (c) & (d); National Monuments Record figs 18 & 47; Library of New College, Oxford fig. 29; Pierpont Morgan Library, New York figs 55(c) & 69; Victoria & Albert Museum figs 3, 20, 30(a), 40 (figs 20, 30(a) & 40 are Crown Copyright); fig. 62 is Crown Copyright, reproduced by permission of the Controller of Her Majesty's Stationery Office.

List of Illustrations

CHAPTER I

FROM TIMBER TO STONE

It has been suggested that if the Saxons had known as much as the Normans did about the siting, building and garrisoning of castles, Duke William might never have conquered and so become King William I of England. Of the few castles known to have existed in this country before 1066, the only really substantial ones were along the Welsh Marches, and these were the handiwork of Norman favourites of Edward the Confessor. But even if the Saxon defences had been many times stronger it is doubtful whether anyone as purposeful as the Conqueror would have been held indefinitely at bay. The most we might venture to suppose is that if the Saxons had possessed anything more secure than a few earthen mounds within wooden or drystone walls, they could conceivably have offered a more protracted resistance and eventually won more favourable terms for themselves.

As it was, William's forces had time after landing to set up temporary forts such as they were skilled in constructing – especially when there were plenty of local captives to do the rough work – and once Harold was defeated they swiftly raised new strongholds to house the occupation troops and keep watch over their new lands.

The Latin word *castellum* means a fortified village or, in a narrower sense, an extensively fortified house which might itself be the focus of a local community. Many British place names derive from such sites: Newcastle upon Tyne neatly defines itself as a town which grew up to serve a new castle beside a river and then grew out from it. In later centuries the word was often grandiosely applied to a manor house 'fortified' with merely decorative embellishments. But in the eleventh century the castle was a starkly functional building, designed and sited for military use; and, at that time, essentially for private military use. British hilltop forts and the *burhs* of Saxons and Danes had been for communal defence. Norman castles were for the king's personal aggrandisement or the personal defence of magnates against rivals or their own discontented peasants.

When William was still only Duke of Normandy he had fortified the town of Caen and established a castle there to safeguard his authority. He followed the same policy in England. Reaching and taking Hastings, his first task was to raise a guardian castle. Impressed by the ease of his own

I
Norman kings displaying some of their architectural achievements: at the top, William the Conqueror with Battle abbey, and William Rufus with Westminster hall; below, Henry I with Reading abbey, and Stephen with Faversham abbey.

11

2
A medieval map of Britain stressing the importance of St Albans abbey in which the cartographer, Matthew Paris, was monk and chronicler, but compressing northern England into an improbable shape and supposing northern Scotland to be an island connected to the mainland only at Stirling.

3
A section of the Bayeux tapestry shows the building of Hastings castle motte.

landing on the shallow Sussex coast near Pevensey, he determined to make it more difficult for any other would-be invader, and another of his early buildings was the castle set within the walls of Anderida, an old Roman fort of the Saxon shore. To give one some sense of the time scale it is worth recalling Jacquetta Hawkes' observation that the Norman building at Pevensey comes just about halfway between the original Roman fortifications and our own day.

The first of these hurriedly erected forts followed a simple basic plan, still to be detected under or within the outlines of even the most complex later strongholds of England and Wales. This was the motte-and-bailey method of construction. The motte was a steep cone of hard-packed earth, flattened at the top. The trench left around its base by the removal of earth for the mound became itself a part of the defence as a dry or wet moat, to which the word 'motte' was later corrupted and transferred. The level summit of the mound was encircled by a stockade of sharpened stakes, and some form of tower would be raised inside, originally of wood but in due course of stone.

A wooden bridge over the ditch joined the motte to its bailey, an enclosure within a double defence of banked-up earthwork and a further loop of ditch. This loop usually connected with the motte ditch to make a figure of eight. Within the bailey were stables, barns, stores and bakehouse, armourers' and farriers' workshops, and living quarters for the lord and his retainers. Access from the outer world was by means of a drawbridge, hauled up at the first sign of approaching danger. If enemies nevertheless succeeded in penetrating the bailey, the defenders fled to their last refuge on the motte, demolishing the inner bridge and wooden steps behind them.

Permanent residence at the top of the mound was neither easy nor desirable. There was little room to move about, sanitary conditions must have been deplorable, and it was a daunting task to carry food up from below and maintain adequate stocks in preparation for an emergency. As soon as a garrison was well settled on a new site, the defences of the bailey were strengthened, not only so that living quarters could be established there but also to lessen its danger of overthrow. The most vulnerable point being the drawbridge gateway, towers were soon installed to command this approach, expanding in later decades into huge gatehouses which were almost fortresses in themselves.

William the Conqueror ordered the erection of military centres at strategic points in his new kingdom: along the vulnerable Channel coast, at gaps in the hills and by river crossings, and in or beside towns and villages whose inhabitants must be dissuaded from the follies of rebellion. At the large motte-and-bailey flung up at Berkhamsted in 1066 the formal surrender of London was received. Soon after his coronation on Christmas Day of that year work began on an earth and timber castle in London itself, to become in due course the Tower of London.

4
(a) The surviving motte-and-bailey outline of Castle Hill, Hallaton, Leicestershire, with 'figure eight' ditches, and (b) the 80-ft high motte and defensive banks of Thetford castle, Norfolk, set on earthworks dating from the Iron Age.

Some of these early buildings were assembled from parts brought over from Normandy in the wake of the invaders, like the prefabricated harbour and bridge sections taken in the Second World War from England to Normandy; and when stone was introduced to make weightier castles, much of it came from William's favoured Caen region. In key townships, blocks of houses were demolished to make way for these royal policing stations. The extent of such clearances can be judged from the fact that Lincoln lost 160 homes, Norwich 113 and, in the words of *Domesday Book* in 1086:

> In the city of York there were 6 shires as well as the archbishop's shire. One shire has been despoiled for castle building.

It was not only the king who built such strongpoints. The barons and prelates who had backed his invasion were granted spacious estates and not merely permission but active encouragement to protect these estates with their own castles, provided they continued to support the king and acknowledge him as ultimate owner of the entire country.

This feudal concept of ownership was quite alien to the Saxons, whose remaining lords soon began to chafe under its restrictions. Their loosely knit way of life had been overwhelmed. Here was no question of a leader as *primus inter pares*, chosen and to some extent controlled by a council of his fellows, but a ruler who imposed himself on the country and its populace as of right.

Wealth in medieval times meant, basically, land. It supported lord and serf alike, at the same time dictating their whole way of life. The king controlled the farming of chosen tracts for his own benefit, and parcelled out the rest among his barons and bishops on the understanding that they were only tenants-in-chief of their ultimate master. Such concessions could be reclaimed by the Crown when the vassal died; though it soon became the custom to hand them on to sons, on payment of a sort of death duty to the king.

Serving these noble tenants as sub-tenants were knights whose duty it was to provide their baron, and through him the king, with 40 days of cavalry service or castle guard each year. In time of war they might be required to serve up to 60 days on horseback, and provide the horse and other necessities at their own expense. Responsibilities of the greater magnates varied. From his wealthy ecclesiastics the king might demand a quota of 50 or 60 armed knights, but those barons charged with manning the turbulent northern and western frontiers were asked to provide only five at a time in order not to weaken their own defences.

The baronial castles themselves must, in time of crisis, be put at royal disposal or handed over for whatever strategic purpose the king considered necessary: a stipulation known as 'rendability'.

This structure of absolute monarch, the privileged, the less privileged and the under-privileged rested upon every man's need for social and military security. The king offered titles and rich estates to his more powerful followers; they in their turn used that power over lesser landowners who contracted to provide services in return for their use of sub-divided lands and grants of certain taxes and perquisites; while below them were subordinates each of whom might own no more than a horse, some armour and weapons, but who in return for loyal duty could expect to be fed and to be respected in war and in the manorial courts. Closest to the earth, slaving to support their immediate superiors and loftier personages up to the apex of the feudal triangle, were a few free but poor farmers, a much larger number of villeins with very limited rights, and serfs who had no rights whatsoever.

Those who in our own time lament the award of peerages, baronetcies, knighthoods and other honours to brewers, financiers, newspaper magnates and show business tycoons, in the romantic belief that such awards in the past were granted only to great heroes and men of impeccable chivalry, should face the probability that most of the great noble families of England are descended from men who licked the right boots or lent their strong right arm to the right usurper at the right time. William the Conqueror, like monarchs before and since, handed out trophies only to fortune hunters who had been shrewd enough to throw in their fortunes with his.

In March 1067 William, feeling that his new kingdom was tolerably secure for the moment, returned to Normandy, leaving his half-brother Odo, bishop of Bayeux, to share the regency with his trusted friend William FitzOsbern. At once, according to the *Anglo-Saxon Chronicle*, these joint administrators made it clear that they would take no chances:

> They built castles far and wide throughout the land, distressing the wretched people, and thereafter things went from bad to worse. May the end be good, when God wills it.

Their methods antagonised those co-operative Saxons who had for a while been reassured by William's promise that he came not as a usurper but as the rightful successor to Edward the Confessor and, at his coronation service in Westminster Abbey following the rite of King Edgar, that he would preserve English laws and customs in the tradition of his predecessors. In his absence there were revolts in many parts of the land. The important coastal fort at Dover held out against a Kentish assault; but attacks on the Norman castle at Hereford inflicted serious damage.

William returned in a mood for vengeance and assembled 'an overwhelming host' to deal with an assault by Harold's sons on Exeter; a rising by the earls of Mercia and Northumbria; and in 1069 a thrust by combined Danish and Northumbrian forces on York, where the Norman castle was destroyed. As a direct result of this, William set about his merciless 'harrying of the north', laying waste the whole region and then rebuilding his castle at York. New and more formidable castles appeared at Exeter, Warwick, Nottingham, Huntingdon and other commanding positions. The breaking of their oath by Saxon lords was punished by final sequestration of their lands. When the *Domesday Book* national survey was prepared 20 years after the Conquest to determine the ownership of property, numbers of employees and liability for taxation and military service, only two estates of any consequence remained in English hands.

* * *

The motte-and-bailey castle had been at best a stop-gap measure. When stone superseded timber in the main construction, it proved difficult to set a building of any great size on top of the earthen mound. A new approach to the geometry of the place was needed. Two developments were those of the shell keep and the great tower keep, defences of last resort just as the motte superstructure had been, but planted on more solid foundations.

A shell keep was basically little more than a single wall or shell enclosing an inner bailey with separate or lean-to buildings, providing living

5
The 12th-century shell keep of Restormel, Cornwall, with domestic and military quarters added within the wall during the 13th century. The projection in the foreground was the chapel.

quarters, storage space, and shelter for those driven in from the outer bailey. Where possible, if too heavy to stand on a man-made hillock, these walls were adapted to natural slopes or outcroppings; and it was essential to choose a site where a well could be sunk within the confines of the keep.

The great tower, usually square or rectangular in its early forms, was a far more massive affair. Too weighty to rest on any ordinary earthwork, it would often be set on a natural vantage point such as that of Peveril, or the Peak, above Castleton in Derbyshire, or even on the level, fenced in by a stone-walled bailey and lesser outbuildings. Where it stood on such low-lying ground a sort of small-scale, steeply pitched motte would sometimes be packed around its lower storey, making direct assault on the fabric itself difficult.

With no entrance at ground level, the lower storey was in effect a capacious cellar used for storage and often for fattening geese and pigs. The main entrance to the building was on the first floor, reached by an outer stairway which, when wooden, could be hauled up if danger threatened, or sheltered within a stone fore-building.

It was customary for the great hall, in which the lord and his retainers spent a large part of their time, to be on this first floor. Sometimes there would be one or two more levels above; but equally often the hall itself would rise the height of two storeys in the centre of the building, with a gallery halfway up from which smaller rooms opened out – rooms which multiplied as the lord's wish for privacy grew greater, or as his family multiplied. Stairs spiralled tightly upwards in one corner of the keep, built into the thick wall or, as defensive corner turrets were added, into one of those turrets. There were few windows, and, as a protective measure, these were little more than narrow slits.

6
Into the old Roman fort of the Saxon Shore at Portchester, Hampshire, Henry II set a great tower whose height was increased during two rebuildings in the following century. It was from here that Henry V set out in 1415 towards victory at Agincourt.

7
William the Conqueror's first castle in London was of earth and timber. In 1077 work began on a rectangular keep of Norman stone which came to be called the White Tower after its whitewashing in the middle of the 13th century. In the days of Henry II, when it was generally referred to as the Palatine castle, one of his sheriffs said of it: 'The walls and keep rise from very deep foundations and are secured with a mortar mixed with beasts' blood.' It has, of course, many other bloody associations. After its spell as a palace with private apartments for the king and his family it became a notorious royal prison, though the more distinguished prisoners were often allowed to have their family and even their servants with them, and to have suitable food and other luxuries sent in from outside.

A feudal lord's home was indeed his castle, as was implied in the more usual name for a keep in its early days: the donjon, a tribute to the *dominus* or lord which in time was debased until a dungeon became simply a dark prison cell, usually underground.

As siege warfare grew more scientific and siege weapons more menacing, straightforward motte-and-bailey or keep-and-bailey construction had to be modified and expanded. At the same time wealthy owners were demanding an improvement in living conditions: more warmth, fewer draughts, better sanitation and the more efficient dispersal of smoke and smells.

To trace these changes one might with advantage trace the architectural history of a castle through the family history of its noble owners – or perhaps through the fortunes of a number of families, since inter-baronial strife and frequent rebellions against various kings meant that buildings tended to change hands abruptly. Descendants of William's loyal barons did not invariably prove loyal to William's own descendants; or, if they did, ran the risk of ending up on the losing side, with obvious results. It is rare to find a castle such as Dunster in Somerset which in nigh on a thousand years has been held by only two families.

Let us take as an example one major contributor to the Norman victory who, originally intended as regent for William's Continental possessions, was brought back to England to help in the suppression of Saxon rebellions. Roger de Monte Comerico – a name which duly became Montgomery – was presented with an earldom comprising some 60,000 acres of Chichester and Arundel, and other properties throughout the kingdom. One of his duties in return was the building of a castle to guard the Arun gap in the South Downs. All that had hitherto existed on the hillside above the river was a Saxon mound with a timber palisade. Roger set to work on a shell keep of stone, with rooms inside for his family and immediate retainers, all their windows facing into the enclosure. The task of watching over the surrounding countryside was shared between feudal tenants conscripted for guard duty and men of his own small garrison.

In the lifetimes of the earl and his successor Arundel keep was further faced with blocks of Caen stone, and a bailey wall was thrust out with a number of heavy buttresses. A deep moat was crossed by a drawbridge, and the gateway for this strengthened by a great gatehouse with a portcullis. Residential buildings, stables and barns grew up within the ward or bailey, and troops were lodged in new towers inserted over the years into the outer walls. Roger also enlarged the town of Arundel until it acquired the status of a borough; and built another castle at Chichester.

When William Rufus became king, his tyrannical behaviour wiped out much of the lingering gratitude felt by many barons towards his father. Even his father's half-brother, bishop Odo, turned against him. Montgomery joined with those who wished to set William II's brother on the throne in his stead. He set off to raise forces from his widespread properties in Shropshire, Staffordshire, Warwickshire and Worcestershire and to subdue the king's supporters, but encountered a serious setback when unable to take Worcester itself. William Rufus, for his part, was unable to take Arundel and began to see that it would be no easy matter to keep the Crown securely on his head unless he could wean the more influential barons away from their fellows. Montgomery's support would be invaluable. King parleyed with earl and they came to terms. One reward for Montgomery's defection and the collapse of the revolt was a royal gift of estates along the Welsh border and deep into Wales itself, eventually to acquire the name of Montgomeryshire. Perhaps the king hoped that by taking on this further grant of distant and troublesome territory the earl would have to stretch his resources so thin and travel so continuously between one outpost and another that he would be unable again to concentrate those resources against his monarch.

8
A Victorian reconstruction of the great hall in Arundel castle. The original hall, built by Richard Fitzalan in the time of Edward III, was completely destroyed during the Parliamentarians' siege of 1643–44.

When Roger died the castle and estate passed to his younger son, who unfortunately also died within a few years, combating a Norwegian invasion of Anglesey. The king allowed the elder brother Robert to take up the inheritance provided a fee of £3,000 was paid into the royal coffers.

Robert continued work on the family property. He added a lower bailey and a new range of domestic buildings, and installed a flanking tower at the only spot where William Rufus's forces had at one stage shown any sign of breaking through. Then he, in his turn, rebelled against his king, but did not fare so well. Henry I, William the Conqueror's fourth son, was much more decisive than William Rufus had been. He besieged Arundel in 1102, and though after three months his men were still unable to penetrate the castle, Robert surrendered. The castle was forfeited to the Crown, and after Henry's death in 1135 became the residence of his widow, who three years later married William de Albini, Lord of Buckingham and Norfolk. It was to her that her step-daughter Matilda came in haste after landing in England to claim the throne.

Henry I's death had left the country without a male heir, his two legitimate sons having been drowned. He had made his barons swear to accept his daughter Matilda as successor, but when the time came they were unhappy at the prospect: she had lived too long abroad, her manner and methods were known to be overbearing, and her second husband, Geoffrey Plantagenet, was a much hated foreigner with blatant designs on Normandy. Instead of honouring their vows, the most powerful men in England swore a fresh allegiance to Henry's nephew, Stephen.

In return the more arrogant of them were greedy for favours. Henry I had broken up some of the more dangerously extensive baronial estates and handed over the castles of defeated rebels to his own favoured officials. Stephen tried to placate the lords and at the same time enlist their support in his dealings with Welsh and Scottish uprisings and with the enraged Matilda and Geoffrey. He failed miserably. The contemptuous barons ran their estates like petty self-contained kingdoms, and throughout the 'nineteen long winters' of his reign seized every opportunity for self-aggrandisement, so that 'the land was all undone and darkened with such deeds, and men said openly that Christ and his angels slept'. The *Anglo-Saxon Chronicle* laments:

Every great man built castles for himself and held them against the king, and they filled all the land with these castles. They sorely burdened the unhappy folk of the country with forced labour on the castles, and when the castles were built they filled them with devils and wicked men. Night and day they seized those whom they believed to have any wealth, whether they were men or women, and in order to get their gold and silver they put them in prison and tortured them with unspeakable tortures, so never were martyrs tortured as they were.

These castles were in general hastily constructed mottes with perhaps a rough-and-ready bailey stockade around wooden shacks. Few were ambitious enough or intended to last long enough to employ stone. Their main purpose was to command enough terrain – it need in some circumstances be no more than a few square miles – to defend the baron's interests, legitimate or otherwise, in the area and to overawe the peasantry. Villagers were harassed into paying what we would now call 'protection money', even when they had little money and almost nothing left worthy of protection. Some fled in the hope of finding a kinder lord. Many died of starvation; many were murdered. The land and people declined until

> one could easily do a day's journey without ever finding a village inhabited or a field cultivated.

In 1139 Stephen, on top of all his other blunders, antagonised the Church by laying siege to some ecclesiastical castles and taking prisoner the bishops. Some of his hard-tried supporters wavered and declared for Matilda when she arrived in England in 1139.

Hearing that Matilda had installed herself at Arundel, the king hurried to besiege the castle. For some reason which has never been satisfactorily explained, in spite of a rash of plausible and not so plausible theories, he did not press the assault but allowed Matilda to leave and stir up passions across the entire countryside. Some of his defecting barons returned to him. It was typical of this shifting and opportunism that in the end a compromise had to be reached: Stephen, his only son having died and there being again no direct heir, should sit on the throne until his death and then bequeath it to Matilda's son Henry of Anjou, who thus became King Henry II.

The Albini family now reaped the reward for its hospitality to Matilda. Her son granted the castle and estates – the 'Honour of Arundel' – to William de Albini and his heirs for ever. The inheritance passed through three more Williams until, the fourth earl dying without male issue, his sister married a Fitzalan, and for some three centuries the estates remained with this family until its union with the Howards.

Other noblemen were less fortunate. Henry II was determined from the outset to bring the barons to heel by demolishing their adulterine, or unlicensed, castles and restricting their rights to fortify their homes. Only under the strictest conditions would the Crown from now on issue a 'licence to crenellate' – that is, to add indented battlements, taking their name from the old French crenel, a notch.

As well as being a demolisher, Henry proved himself a great builder in his own interest. Royal exchequer records show him and his two successors, Richard I and John, spending so much on castle work that it was repeatedly the largest single item in their annual budget. Tower keeps went up all over the land: square as at Bamburgh, Appleby and Dover;

multiangular at Orford; and – a new departure – a number of cylindrical keeps.

The most famous of the round towers is that at Windsor, set on a solid mound which had previously borne a wooden building. The advantages of such construction were mainly military: there were no corners for attackers to pick away at or undermine, and no 'blind spots' which defenders could not cover. William Marshal, Henry's trusted earl of Chepstow and tutor to his son Henry, emulated the royal technique by inserting circular towers into the walls of Chepstow castle and building a massive round keep at Pembroke.

Although the Conqueror and his descendants formally required military service in return for land and other favours granted to their vassals, it had early become the custom of those with other preoccupations to offer a payment of scutage – 'shield tax' – in place of actual physical service. Henry II found that it made good sense to apply part of this income to the hiring of a regular army of mercenaries, backed up by a national militia when necessary. To be sure that everyone paid his full dues, he ordered the preparation of records in as much detail as *Domesday Book*, whose basic facts and figures had long since become confused and were now in need of reassessment. Henry wanted to know just what feudal service was owed to him, what his tenants were drawing from their sub-tenants, and what scutage he could require from those whose 'knight service' was commuted or not really needed for the specified number of days each year. For example, one of his lords, Richer de Laigle of Pevensey, respectfully reported:

> Know that I have 35 knights' fees and a half, and I had so many on the day and in the year that King Henry your grandfather lived and died. Nor have I enfeoffed any since that day. These figures are correct:
> Richard, son of William holds 15 knights' fees
> Ralph of Dene, 6 knights
> William Malet, 4 knights' fees
> William son of Richard, 3 knights' fees
> William Malfed, 3 knights
> William of Echingham, 2 knights
> Robert of Horsted, 2 knights
> Andreas of Alfriston, half a knight

The 'Honour of Arundel' had been calculated in William I's time as containing $89\frac{1}{2}$ knights' fees. By Henry II's time the estates must have represented something far richer. Albini remained a favourite and when, one by one, Henry's own sons turned against him, it was the earl who commanded the king's army in Normandy against them.

After a humiliating defeat by the king of France, Henry lamented that his own flesh and blood had brought shame on him and prophesied that of all

9
Henry II's keep at Orford, Suffolk, with a circular plan inside but a polygonal exterior, has three spacious floors, a chapel, and a number of smaller rooms in the turrets. The castle of which this is the only surviving building was set up as a guardian not merely against the king's enemies from over the water but against the perpetually rebellious Bigod barons, on a previously unfortified site. Stone was shipped from Caen, and timber – some of which can still be traced in the defences – from Yorkshire. Flanking fire from the turrets could cover the whole main face of the tower.

of them his favourite son John would 'do more harm than all the others in the end'. He died in 1189, leaving the fundamentally efficient country which he had built up after the disasters of Stephen's rule to be plunged into turmoil once more.

In the ten years of his reign Richard I was to spend only ten months in his kingdom. He finished the work his father had begun on Dover castle, but his own favourite castle was not in England: it was the superb Château Gaillard on a cliff commanding the Seine south of Rouen. When asserting his feudal right of armed backing for a campaign in Normandy against Philip Augustus of France, Richard took the custom of scutage a stage further by stipulating that each of his lords should send only seven knights and provide the balance in cash to help pay for the war. Glad to be left with the majority of their henchmen still on local call, the noble landlords gladly accepted the arrangement.

Richard's absences, however, laid up other trouble for the country. Such financial assets as he had left behind after satisfying his demands for support in France and the Holy Land were preyed on by his scheming brother John, whose extortions grew worse when he himself came to the throne.

10
Chepstow castle, set on a rock commanding a river crossing of strategic importance from Roman times onwards where the Wye at times produces the highest tides in the British Isles, has three baileys. A gatehouse, the great hall and Marten's Tower, called after a prisoner who spent 20 years in captivity in it, are in the foreground, with the rectangular great tower on the narrowest part of the ridge.

Castle building went on, both by the new king and by barons no longer under the restraining eye of Henry II. King John managed to lose his brother's beloved Château Gaillard, and with it all of Normandy. At home he ordered improvements to the castle of Worcester, a town for which he had a particular affection and where by his own request he was ultimately buried. He seized private castles on the flimsiest excuses, such as those at Pontefract and Knaresborough; and also took over Kenilworth, which with only a few breaks was now to remain in royal hands until the sixteenth century. Kenilworth had been dismantled in his father's reign, but retained its impressive tower keep and a fine water defence which, produced by damming the near-by river, was more like a lake than a moat. The impressive outer curtain wall, with its towers and sturdy buttresses, was largely John's work. At Odiham he ordained an entirely new castle with an octagonal keep. Also he had reason to be grateful for the rebuilding programme carried out by his father and his brother Richard at Dover which, as in the days of King William I, held out against a desperate enemy assault in the last turbulent year of John's reign.

Disgusted by John's failures on the Continent and his rapacity at home,

11
Pembroke castle, dominated by William Marshal's circular keep of 1200. Protected on three sides by water, the stronghold, though in Wales, was basically an English castle protecting English interests. In 1457 it was the birthplace of the sole surviving Lancastrian claimant to the throne from the Wars of the Roses, eventually to become King Henry VII.

12
Dover castle has within its hilltop courtyard a Roman lighthouse beside a Saxon church. Henry II's keep is nearly 100 feet square and 90 feet high, with walls 22 feet thick at the base. Water from a well within the keep was piped to many of the rooms. The outer curtain wall belongs largely to the 13th century, with the massive Constable's Tower replacing an earlier, weaker gateway almost overcome by French attackers.

13
The 12th-century rectangular keep of Kenilworth was known as Caesar's Tower. The curtain walls belong to the next century, and the great hall to the one after that when John of Gaunt remodelled the fortress as a palace. Here Elizabeth I's favourite Robert Dudley, earl of Leicester, laid out pleasure gardens and lavishly entertained the queen. After Charles I's execution there was talk of demolishing the castle entirely in case it should provide a focus for further Royalist resistance, but in the end it was merely 'slighted'.

the barons had been complaining about sequestration of their properties and the loss of many old privileges, and to their delight found a most respectable ally. In the company of Stephen Langton, whose papal appointment as Archbishop of Canterbury the king had vainly resisted, they swore at the high altar of Bury St Edmunds on St Edmunds Day 1214 that they would force from John a Great Charter confirming their feudal rights and settling their grievances. John was forced to put his seal to Magna Carta at Runnymede in June 1215.

But he was a bad loser. In no time at all he was at odds with his barons

14
King John's seal, used on Magna Carta.

once more – goaded, it must be conceded, by the arrogance of those who now considered they were free to build more castles where it suited them and to pillage royal estates.

When John died in 1216 his son came to the throne as Henry III at the age of nine. In spite of weaknesses of character which seemed all too direct an inheritance from his father, an equal greed for extortionate taxation and bungled wars, and the continuing problem of baronial strife which his father had failed to subdue, Henry ruled for 56 years.

While still in his teens he took command of a punitive expedition against one of his father's favourites. A loyal supporter of King John, Fawkes de Bréauté, had received among other rewards Bedford castle, confiscated from William de Beauchamp. In this new reign Beauchamp urged the young king's counsellors to recognise him as rightful owner, but although they agreed with this claim the sitting tenant, de Bréauté, refused to hand over the property. Worse, in one of his absences, a royal judge was kidnapped by the castellan and held in custody. The 17-year-old Henry now took a hand, personally laying siege to the castle and taking the Archbishop of Canterbury with him to pronounce sentence of excommunication on those who thus defied the king. When the castle finally succumbed after two months it was as the result of a classic sequence: breaching the bailey, driving the defenders into the keep on its motte, mining a corner of the tower and smoking them out. The leaders were hanged. Beauchamp's property was restored to him, though not in very good condition: the main defences had been razed to the ground, the stones

15
Henry III issuing instructions for a new building project.

16
Clifford's Tower, a 13th-century addition to the original York castle set on a Norman motte.

given to local churches, and all that remained was a residential range within the inner bailey.

Henry's attitude to his own castles introduced some amelioration of living conditions. Just as he directly encouraged the new trends in ecclesiastical architecture which were producing the glories of Early English and Gothic, and personally laid down the criteria for rebuilding Westminster Abbey, so he instigated a more aesthetic approach – and at the same time aimed at greater physical comfort – to the fittings and decorations of hitherto purely functional fortresses. After his marriage he carried out extensive improvements at Windsor, and more after the birth of his son Edward. Winchester castle blossomed with new residential quarters, fine tiles and wall painting. One wonders if it was he who obliterated the prophetic design commissioned there by his grandfather of an eagle whose four sons were gathering to pick out its eyes. Now the king and queen each had a separate chapel, and special care was lavished on the fine castle hall which is all that remains of the building in our present century.

It was unfortunate that Henry's artistic good taste did not carry over into his political ideas. When Simon de Montfort, born into an ancient French family, came to England in 1231 to claim the earldom of Leicester he soon became one of Henry's favourites and married his sister Eleanor. Appointed Governor of Gascony, he later served as one of the king's most trusted ambassadors. But, efficient and puritanical himself, de Montfort came to deplore Henry's shiftiness and incompetence. Resolute in urging that the neglected principles of Magna Carta should be implemented, he finally threw in his lot with those barons who were once again preparing to defy the Crown.

In 1258 the Provisions of Oxford transferred most of the king's administrative functions to a baronial council. But Henry appealed to the

17
The seal of Simon de Montfort.

Pope, won his support, and worked against the barons now endeavouring to rule the country until civil war was inevitable. In 1264 Henry was defeated and captured at Lewes, together with his son Edward. The following year Edward escaped and, facing a de Montfort weakened by withdrawal of the support of many disaffected barons, killed him at the battle of Evesham.

Some 22 years earlier Henry had given Kenilworth castle into the keeping of de Montfort and his wife, the king's sister. Now the second son of the family, another Simon, tried to hold on to it, sending his men out on regular sorties for food and loot from the surrounding countryside. When a royal army came to lay siege to the castle, Simon fled to France in the vain hope of raising support there. The defenders he had left behind held out for six months, but then were forced to surrender rather than starve.

Reassertion of royal authority was so surprisingly successful that there were no serious upsets during the rest of Henry's reign. Prince Edward not only deemed it safe to leave his father's side and go off on a Crusade, but after Henry's death in 1271 remained abroad for two years before returning to ascend his throne.

*　　　*　　　*

Looking back at the family we left in possession of Arundel, we find that the last Albini died in 1243, when the castle passed through marriage to John Fitzalan of Clun and Oswestry, the remainder of the 'Honour' to Geoffrey de Langley. John was to be succeeded by six earls of Arundel in direct descent. During their tenure the castle was twice forfeited to the Crown, but each time restored.

In the year of Edward I's accession the son of John Fitzalan had just died, leaving the inheritance to a five-year-old grandson. As this boy,

Richard, grew up it became more and more obvious that major repairs were needed to large tracts of the castle. To help raise the necessary funds Richard received the grant of a royal fair in Arundel, together with a patent authorising him to overhaul the town defences in general. He rebuilt the upper part of his gatehouse and added an outer gateway, served by a drawbridge and flanked by two high towers and dungeons deep below ground.

Richard was to become a favourite at Edward I's court, and his son Edmund was knighted at the same time as the king's son, later Edward II. The friendship between the two young men had an unhappy outcome. When Queen Isabella turned against Edward II, who was to meet such a hideous death in Berkeley castle, her lover Mortimer captured Arundel and had Edmund beheaded.

After the male line of the Fitzalan earls ended, the holding and title passed by marriage into the powerful Howard family, dukes of Norfolk, whose male descendants still hold their titles and that of Earl Marshal of England.

Through the centuries there were further additions to the building, and many softening influences. A modern plan shows features which would have surprised its early medieval occupants: library, billiard room, drawing room, dining room and breakfast room. What it lacks is the most characteristic single chamber of all medieval castles and manors, combining all the functions of drawing, dining and breakfast rooms. The great hall at Arundel, built during the reign of Edward III, was completely destroyed during a Parliamentary siege in the seventeenth century. In many other locations such halls survive to evoke for us the communal domestic life of the times.

CHAPTER II

FAMILY AND RETAINERS

Through many generations the great hall was the centre of all castle life, shared by the lord and the majority of his household. Here the business of the estate was largely transacted, here men, women and children slept, and here they ate together. 'It is not seemly,' decreed a medieval book on etiquette, 'that a lord should eat alone.'

Waking in the morning, the lord and his lady would find themselves in their bed at one end of the hall, usually at the back of the dais, curtained off from the rest. Or perhaps they were among the pioneers of what later became customary: a small private chamber partitioned off from the main body of the hall or even recessed into the wall of the keep, with wainscoting and some painted panelling to distinguish it from the whitewashed walls elsewhere. If the hall was of the two-storey variety, family bedrooms could be set behind the gallery, and from his solar above the dais the lord was in a position to study activities in the great space below.

Lesser members of his household slept on benches along the walls, upon straw-filled palliasses, or simply on a carpet of rushes and herbs on the floor, pulling cloaks or rugs about them. Since, in spite of regular shifting and replacing, these rushes were all too likely to be impregnated with the grease and spillage from the food consumed in the hall, and with the droppings of favourite dogs and falcons who were present at mealtimes, such a couch must have been none too salubrious. Even in the lord's private recess, carpets were a rarity until well into the thirteenth century, and other luxuries were equally scarce. Tapestries gradually made their appearance, combining pleasant decoration with the need to combat draughts. Early halls had an open fire in the middle of the floor; and even when fireplaces were built into the walls, proper chimneys were unknown until the late thirteenth century, so that the primitive flues driven through the walls combined with draughts from the unglazed windows to swirl a great deal of smoke about, soon discolouring the whitewash.

The household rose early. The first duty was attendance at mass in the chapel – a small chamber in most early castles, before it became fashionable to sponsor more and more elaborate chapels as prestige symbols. When larger buildings could safely be built within the confines of a reasonably

33

18
The great hall within the keep
of Castle Hedingham, Essex.

secure bailey, many included a crypt in which generations of the family would be buried. It was rare, though, in Norman times to find anything quite as ambitious as the domestic chapel within the keep at Castle Rising in Norfolk.

Mass was said by the lord's chaplain, or – from the word 'chancel' – chancellor. He would also say grace before meals, and attend to his master's personal and official correspondence.

The first meal of the day was spartan for most: usually a hunk of bread and a pot of ale before work commenced; though the baron himself might have white wheaten bread and a slice of cold meat, perhaps even a glass of wine. While his servants went about their duties, the baron and his steward would then settle down to administrative matters in the hall. Tenants arrived with rents or respectful complaints, submitting local disputes for judgment. There might be ticklish matters of inheritance to settle, or deaths

or marriages to discuss. When a knightly sub-tenant died and the son wished to take over, the lord could claim a fee which might be as much as the first year's income from the relevant holdings. He might also wish to suggest a suitable match for the dead man's widow; or, if the heir was still a minor, could act as guardian and work out what extra profits this would entitle him to from the estate. If his own son were to be knighted, he expected contributions towards expenses from his vassals. If his daughter married, a wedding donation was imperative.

There were two complementary divisions in the household: one military, the other administrative. The military included knights in the magnate's service, stabling their horses in the bailey under the care of a stable marshal, and the numerous squires, men-at-arms, castle watchmen, archers and crossbowmen, and sub-tenants doing a spell of service as sentries along the battlements. Smiths and carpenters maintained the more

19
John of Gaunt's hall in Kenilworth.

20
A law-giver exhausted by his day's work.

advanced engines of war; farriers attended to the horses. Not all of these would be simultaneously or permanently on the premises, save in some royal castles built specifically to defend strategic points and keep constant watch over the more unsettled parts of the realm. Rather than keep expensive standing garrisons, it was more usual practice to call on men to fulfil their feudal duties only when an emergency loomed.

At the head of the other section was the steward or major-domo. Originally his responsibilities took in both the domestic routine and the management of his master's rural estates, but in the case of a baron whose power and possessions were growing it became common to sub-divide these functions. One steward or seneschal took over indoor matters, the other went out of doors.

The domestic staff lived in a hierarchy as clearly marked out as that of their overlord's fuedal obligations. Close to the steward, and sometimes combining the steward's duties with his own, was the chamberlain, responsible for the whole organisation supplying the great chamber, or hall. There was an usher on duty at the door of the hall. The cook worked in a team which was to survive in similar form through many centuries into Victorian days, and even beyond.. There was a pantler, or officer in charge of the pantry, taking his name from the French *pain*, or bread; the butler (bottler) supervising the buttery where drink was kept in butts or bottles; and a butcher, baker and – quite literally – candlestick maker. There were maids, skivvies, and stable lads. And with seamstresses and laundresses at his command there was the highly esteemed keeper of the wardrobe.

In the baronial court, often entrusted with its entire supervision in the absence of his lord, the estates seneschal would sit with the chaplain or his clerk beside him to take notes and prepare documents. He kept full accounts of the manors within the baronial domain and their output in food, timber, service or taxes, and toured them several times a year. According to a thirteenth-century treatise on *Husbandrie*, a qualified seneschal

should have lands of demesne measures, should know by the perch of the country how many acres in each field for sowing (wheat, rye, barley, oats, peas, beans and dredge), ploughing (each plough should plough 9

21
A wall fireplace in the King's Gate at Caernarvon.

22
The richly ornamented Norman upper chapel, one of two, in the forebuilding to the keep of Dover castle.

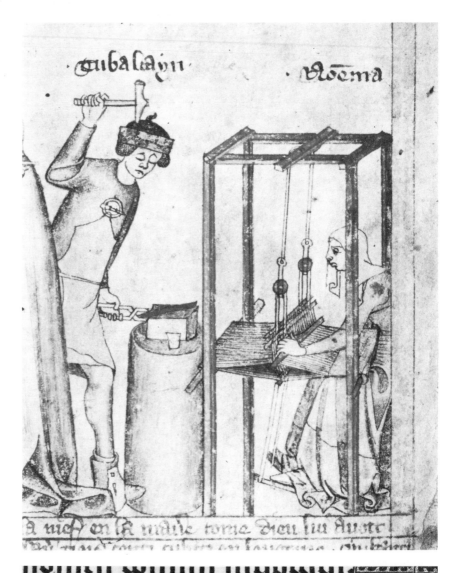

23
Metalwork and weaving.

24
A knight and his entourage at table. The scene comes from the Luttrell Psalter, an illuminated manuscript created for a 14th-century Lincolnshire knight, Sir Geoffrey Luttrell.

score acres – 60 for winter seed, for spring seed and in fallow), also how many acres to be ploughed by boon custom and how many by the desmesne ploughs; reaping (how many acres by boon and custom and how many for money), meadows and pastures (how much hay is needed, how much stock can be kept on pastures and on common). Also how stock is kept and improved. Fines imposed if loss or damage due to want of guard. No under or over stocking of manors. If lord needs money for debts, Seneschal should see from which manor he can have money at greatest advantage and smallest loss.

The 'boon' mentioned in this passage refers to the donation of free service at special times required from a tenant or villein by his lord.

When the morning's business had been transacted in the hall, the main meal of the day was forthcoming, at what may seem to us the disconcertingly early hour of ten or eleven o'clock. Trestle tables were set up and laid with silver for the lord and his lady on their dais, earthenware vessels and horn or wooden implements for the others. While his retainers sat on the benches which some of them had used for sleeping the night before, the lord and lady might use chairs – imposing but heavy, and through most of the Norman period lacking such comforts as upholstery.

The chaplain said grace. The food was brought in. Because of the difficulty of disposing of smoke and smells, a great deal of cooking was almost certainly done out in the open when weather permitted. Kitchens might be incorporated in buildings against one of the bailey walls, or on the lower floor of the keep with ovens and fireplaces set in the walls, but either way the food was unlikely to arrive very hot at the table after traversing the draughty courtyards or being carried up spiral stone staircases.

The estate and its tenants supplied many ingredients for the various dishes, but in addition there were imported luxuries such as wine and the spices essential to disguise the flavour of bad and rancid meat, fish or soups. With no means of preserving meat other than by salting it down, the practice wherever possible was to eat an animal within a day or so of its being slaughtered; but salting was essential to ensure supplies throughout the winter, since the efficacy of root crops as winter feed had not yet been discovered, or to keep the inmates from starvation during a siege.

There was no lack of variety in foodstuffs. Beef, mutton, pork and bacon were as familiar then as now, though not so plentiful for the man in the street – or in the fields. Much of it had to be stewed rather than grilled or roasted since it came from tough animals ranging more energetically and fed a less calculated balanced diet than ours. Some of the rest was powdered or minced into a paste with milk, herbs and breadcrumbs, not unlike a modern rissole. Birds such as starlings, pigeons and gulls were more acceptable on the table then, along with peacocks and herons, and larks' tongue pie was a great delicacy. Of course there was a great deal of game in

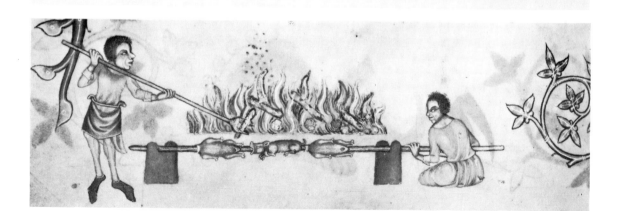

25
(a, b & c) Preparing food for boiling in cauldrons and rotating on a spit; (d) the kitchen of Berkeley castle.

castles near the preciously preserved hunting forests: venison was roasted or, like other viands, ground to paste by pestle and mortar.

Most of the fruits and vegetables of our own day were available, apart from potatoes and tomatoes – onions, peas, beans, cabbages, leeks, apples and pears among them – though in some quarters they were looked down on as peasants' fare. Herbs and a number of vegetables could be grown in a kitchen garden within the castle precincts. A typical salad would include parsley, sage, garlic, leeks, borage, mint, fennel, purslayne, rosemary and rue, dressed with oil, salt and vinegar or with verjuice – the acid juice of crab apples, also used as a liquor for cooking meat.

Butter and cheese were brought in from the estate or sometimes made on the premises, often from ewes' or goats' milk. The miller ground flour for delivery in sacks to the castle baker. Anything lacking in the immediate vicinity was purchased from merchants who could guarantee seasonal supplies of herring, fruit, spices, and delicacies such as wine, figs and raisins.

At table a thick slice of bread was commonly put in the bottom of a bowl, and then soup or stew poured over it, or a paste of minced meat spread on it. More solid pieces of meat, carved from a joint or bird roasted on the spit, would customarily be served on to the silver plate of the lord or the flat wooden platters of his retainers, and eaten with the fingers. Here again, a slice of bread might if wished be set on the platter as a foundation – a sort of

Domestic equipment: (a) a 'face jug,' c. 1300, with a groove making it possible to pour liquid from the tip of the nose; (b) a bronze cooking pot; (c) a hook for lifting meat out of a cauldron; (d) a pair of kitchen shears, used more commonly than scissors.

primitive open sandwich – or a slice of stale bread from the previous day could itself serve as platter.

Wine from the barrel was poured into jugs and served at the top table, while the lower orders contented themselves with ale brewed by the resident ale-wife. In this at least they were at one with the folk of field and village: even the humblest cottagers brewed their own ale or cider in those days.

A couple of recipes which have been handed down to us may or may not whet the twentieth-century appetite:

LAMPREYS IN GALYTYNE – Take lamprey and skin him with vinegre and salt. Skald him in water. Slytte him and take the guttes out at the end. Kepe the bloode. Put ye lamprey on a spytt. Rost him and keep the greece. Grinde raysons and mix them with vinegre and crusts of bread. Add thereto powder gynger and ye bloode and ye greece. Boyl ye sauce and salte it.

AN ENTRAYLE – Take a sheepis stomache. Take pullets roasted and hew them to pieces. Then take pork, cheese, and spicery, and put it in a mortar and grynde it all fyne. Then take uppe the egges hard boyld, and put it in the stomache with salte, and boyle it till it be enough, and serve it forthe.

During Lent the Church forbade the eating of meat, and in those days the Church's dictates rang more formidably than now. Many castles, like the monasteries, had their own fishponds, or used the moat for this auxiliary purpose. Local rivers might supplement the diet. But local supplies were rarely enough to last through the fasting period, and vast consignments of salted herring had to be transported from the coast. This trade was of the greatest significance for the fishing ports through which it was channelled. In return for guaranteed supplies, calculated as sternly as scutage and tithe and the boon work and feudal service owed by those who lived and worked inland, the fishermen were exempted from many of the obligations which weighed on those who tilled the soil. So many concessions had been made to the East Anglian and south-east coast communities by the time of Richard II, including freedom from appropriation of their boats for national service or official voyages, that many farm lads left the oppressions of the land and moved out to farm the sea.

Salt, so important for the preservation of fish and meat, made those who worked the mines and saltpans people of some consequence, able to do profitable deals with the owners of great estates. One thirteenth-century document prepared on behalf of the Earl of Chester by his clerk records such a contract:

27
Netting fish – supposedly a representation of Edward II enjoying the company of Fenland watermen.

Know that I have given and granted and by this present charter of mine have confirmed to Thomas of Croxton for his homage and service half a salthouse of the fee of Ralph Brereton which Gilbert, chaplain of Middlewich, gave me, as well as all the land which Erneis the chaplain

held between the estate of William Brun and the brook which runs close to the earl's bakehouse.

One notes the usual feudal requirement of 'homage and service'.

At the end of dinner, whether the main course had been meat, fowl, or good red herring, the chaplain's almoner would collect such bones and scraps as had not been tossed to the dogs, and bread left soaking in the bottom of soup bowls. It was his duty to visit the poor and distribute these scraps, and also

> to receive discarded horses, clothing, money and other gifts, bestowed in alms, and to distribute them faithfully. He ought also by frequent exhortations to spur the king to liberal almsgiving, especially on saints' days, and to implore him not to bestow his robes . . . upon players, flatterers, fawners, talebearers or minstrels, but to command them to be used to augment his almsgiving.

Assuming that the lord of the castle was today spared any such exhortation from his almoner, and that there was no further pressing business to attend to, his mind might well turn to the prospect of an afternoon's hunting. The best days of all were those when there were no administrative duties to be performed and he could set out in the early morning for a whole day in the forest, with a picnic meal to be served during a lull in the chase. Today his treasured falcon had probably been

28
Hunting the deer.

sitting hooded on the back of his chair throughout the meal, and now it was high time to exercise him – or her, for the male tiercel was far less aggressive and less favoured than the female falcon.

To a nobleman, hawking was perhaps the dearest of all aspects of the chase. Deer and wild boar might be pursued avidly through the forests, with the more adventurous ladies accompanying the hunt; but the skilled falconer was the aristocrat of huntsmen, and the falcon more precious than any hunting dog. Animals on the ground could be cornered or worn out before the kill. Birds were more enticingly elusive. There were as yet no guns to massacre them in mid-air, and they could swiftly wing their way out of arrow range. Winged predators had to be trained to swoop on them and bring them down. Training was arduous both for the hawk and hawker, and when it was completed the birds were looked after with the greatest devotion in the castle mews.

William I, said to have 'loved the tall deer as if he had been their father', preserved them for his own sport. Anyone who without royal permission killed a hart or a hind was blinded. Peasants who in Saxon times had supplied themselves with kindling and small game from the woods had been banned from certain areas set aside for royal diversion, but now in Norman times found themselves deprived of almost all such facilities in growing expanses of forest and open country. Feudal forest law permitted the wholesale demolition of villages and hamlets within game reserves set aside for exclusive royal or baronial use. Verderers' courts enforced the harshest penalties on a hungry man who touched as much as a rabbit. Poachers were hanged or mutilated, and anyone who raised the mildest protest against the verderers was liable to be deprived of all his possessions. The only concessions were to warreners who helped keep down hares, badgers, foxes, and other animals thought to be harmful to the more highly valued game. Even so-called 'free warren' was a perk for the lord or minor gentry rather than the needy peasant, being yet another of those things which could be won from the king in return for payment or service. It has more than once been pointed out that the adjective 'free' in any medieval transaction generally meant the freedom of one member of the community to oppress others.

On return from the chase the lord might take a bath. Water was poured into a wooden tub in his bedchamber or curtained recess, and he sat in it upon a stool. The soap used would have been made on the premises from meat fat, wood ash and soda, unless he was prepared to import expensive soap from Mediterranean countries, made with an olive oil base and perfumed with herbs.

Shaving must have been an uncomfortable operation with knife blades which, by our standards, were surely jagged and liable to rasp the skin.

As to our usual adjunct to the bathroom, the privy or garderobe, this was set into an outer wall or even built out over a shaft which might end in a

29
Setting off for a day's hawking.

ditch, in the moat, or, ideally, in running water. Sometimes a number of latrines on different floors fed into such a shaft, the deposits being cleaned out at intervals by some unfortunate serf. In hot weather or after the visit of a king's or fellow nobleman's retinue, or during a siege, the smell within the castle must have been a sore trial. Sanitation in even the most exalted households left much to be desired. Henry III once objected so strongly to the stench in the Tower of London that before returning to it from his travels he adjured the constable:

> Since the privy in the chamber of our wardrobe at London is situated in an undue and improper place, wherefore it smells badly, we command you on the faith and love by which you are bounden to us that you in no wise omit to cause another privy chamber to be made . . . even though it should cost a hundred pounds.

After completing his ablutions, and as twilight fell, the lord presided over his ménage at supper. This was a less substantial meal than dinner unless there were a special feast with visitors to be impressed and diverted.

In his absence during the afternoon his wife and other ladies of the castle had perhaps worked on their embroidery, gossiped and told tales or riddles, thereafter joining the children when the tutor had released them. Children and adults shared much the same romps and pastimes, including 'hoodman blind' and other variations on blind-man's-buff, skipping and dancing games, and various simple dice games. The more skilled devoted themselves to chess or forms of billiards and backgammon. After supper

30
Indoor games:
(a) a move at chess;
(b) judging from their expressions, a few gamblers have lost heavily on the dice.

31
(a) Musicians entertaining at dinner.
(b) The high arch of the bow was normal for centuries in playing instruments of the viol family, until the introduction of the straighter stick with which we are nowadays familiar.

they might continue in the same mood with the lord joining them or, if he was exhausted by the business and outdoor exercise of his day, retiring to a chamber where some of the ladies might wait on him, flirt with him, and perhaps play music. In the hall other musicians were perhaps tuning up – strolling players to entertain the household and accompany an hour or so of dancing.

With darkness settled down outside, the interior was lit by candles made from wax or animal fat rendered down and then solidified, set on iron-spiked candlesticks or in wall brackets which also held torches of resinous wood or rushlights made from dipping twisted strands of rush into grease or tallow. A portable lantern with its candle shielded by translucent slices of horn was used when negotiating draughty passages or staircases.

When it was time to call an end to the evening, the captain of the guard would ensure that the sentries were properly posted and alert, and the lord and lady retired to their room, said their prayers, hung up their clothes . . . and so to bed.

*   *   *

In such chill surroundings it was usual to dress warmly rather than stylishly. Men wore thick cloth or woollen stockings, sometimes simply extensions of a sort of combination under-garment, covered with tunics or cloaks reaching almost to the ground. In moments of relaxation a noble might don a fine woollen or linen tunic with sleeves narrowing to the wrist, and over this a shorter sleeveless tunic belted at the waist. His lady's long-sleeved tunic, girdled at the waist and perhaps with a gold, silver or jewelled clasp, might sport sleeves wider from shoulder to forearm; and as

32
*Gold and jewellery:
(a) a late 12th-century gold
signet ring; (b) three 14th-
century English silver brooches;
(c) early 14th-century gold
ornament with emeralds, pearls
and sapphires.*

time went on a number of extravagances appeared in the sleeves, sprouting long hangings from the wrist or elbow. Women's trim headgear – a white veil in the twelfth century, a folded wimple held in place by a stiff cap in the thirteenth – blossomed through the fourteenth century into the awe-inspiring extravagances of the fifteenth. As living conditions grew less austere, so clothing became less austere and more mannered, lighter to wear and easier to cut and shape into imaginative designs. Head-dresses (by no stretch of the language could they be called hats) rose into lofty gilded cones which must have presented problems when the wearer passed under a low lintel, or aped a bishop's mitre with constructions of velvet, brocade, embroidery, golden threads and precious stones. Men, too, indulged increasingly in coxcomb flamboyance: tight-waisted tunics, fur collars and cuffs, and, for indoor wear, long leather shoes which remind one of the much derided 'winkle-pickers' of the mid-twentieth century. Sexual suggestiveness, romantic and flirtatious display, have combined into many patterns, postures and colours throughout the centuries; but the basic drama has remained much the same, even if the relative roles of hero and heroine are no longer as ill balanced as they once were.

In the Middle Ages a girl might be betrothed at the age of nine or ten and married well before her fourteenth birthday. Many parents pressed for early marriage in order to avoid possible depredations to their estates if the father, or both of them, should die before the child came of age. Yet another of the Crown's sources of feudal income was the guardianship of orphaned minors, which could be sold or leased out at a profit to some other lord; and, as we have seen, local magnates had a financial interest in local widows and juvenile heirs.

33
*Costumes of (a) the 14th
century and (b & c) the 15th
century.*

When ordering the compilation of records of royal dues throughout the land, Henry II did not omit to order the inclusion of widows and heirs under such wardship in case there might be some tax outstanding or some profitable investment overlooked. Even ladies of the greatest consequence found it hard to avoid the dictates of their guardian, especially when the king was nominally that guardian. Richard I, greedy as ever to subsidise one of his foreign expeditions, decided to collect the fee due to him on the marriage of the Earl of Essex's widow, and commanded her to marry a man he had picked out for her. She desired no such marriage; but the king made it clear that if she refused he would confiscate all her possessions, so in the end she had to submit.

Marriages of convenience were the rule rather than the exception. Desirable liaisons were encouraged by sending daughters of the family away to the castles of other noble families for their education. Failing a deliberate plan of this kind, the girls were sometimes tucked away and educated in a convent until a suitable bridegroom was found. If none was forthcoming or if they found their true vocation in the convent itself, they often remained there.

Unmarried, the young woman was her father's chattel. Once married, no matter how great the dowry she took with her, she became her husband's chattel. He could use her property and her body as it pleased him, and could strike her not merely with impunity but with the tacit approval of friends and relations if he felt she needed chastisement or encouragement. In time of outrageous wrong the lady might appeal to influential kinsfolk for help against him, but it was rare for this to happen.

If was the wife's duty to take good care of the household and even to familiarise herself with the duties of the seneschal, no matter how trusted he might be, so that, though supposedly of inferior sex, she should be able to stand in for her lord, since of so many women it could be said that 'often they dwell at home without their husbands, who are at court or in divers lands'. Divers lands indeed: many were called upon to accompany their king on Crusade, or even to go in his place; others served in repetitive dynastic wars in France and Normandy; some were often abroad slyly negotiating favours for themselves and their estates with would-be usurpers whose cause it might prove prudent to espouse.

In spite of her legal disabilities the lady could not, then, afford to be forever meek and downtrodden. Matilda had proved a formidable claimant to the throne in Stephen's time, and even those without royal blood in their veins often proved as knowledgeable and courageous as their menfolk. They were often better read and with wider interests, in spite of being shut away for so much of the time while their husbands roved the outside world.

A striking example of a woman's victory on behalf of her husband and his property is that of the wife of Sir John de Pelham, constable of Pevensey castle in the time of Richard II. John had decided to support the cause of the exiled Henry Bolingbroke, and in his absence on campaign the king's supporters moved in to seize Pevensey. During the siege the châtelaine wrote 'To my trew Lorde':

> My dere Lord, I recommande me to your hie Lordeschipp wyth hert & body, & all my pore myght; and wyth all this I think zow, as my dere Lorde, derest & best yloved of all erthlyche Lordes; I say for me, and thanke yhow, my dere Lord, with all thys that I say before, off your comfortable lettre that ze send me from Pownefraite that com to me on Mary Magdaleyn day; ffor by my trowth I was never so gladd as when I herd by your lettre that ye warr stronge ynogh, wyth the grace off God, for to kepe you fro the malyce of your ennemys ... And my dere Lord iff it lyk zow for to know off my ffare, I am here by layd in manner off a sege, with the counté of Sussex, Sudray, & a great parcyll off Kente, so that I ne may noght out nor none vitayles gette me, bot wt myche hard. Wharfore my dere iff it lyk zow, by the awyse off zowr wyse counsell, for to sett remedye off the salvation off yhower Castell, and wtstand the malyce off thes schires forsayde. And also that ye be fullyche enformed off these grett malce wyrkers in these schyres whych yt haffes so dispytffully wrogth to zow, and to zowr castell, to yhowr men, and to zour tenants, ffore this cuntree have yai wastede, for a gret whyle. Farewele my dere Lorde; the Holy Trinyté zow kepe fro zour ennemys, and son send me gud tythings off yhow.
>
> Ywrten at Pevensay in the castell on Saynt Jacobe day last past,
>
> By yhowr awnn pore
>
> J. PELHAM

The lady Pelham seems, however, to have been far from poor in spirit. It was not just the defence of the castle which was noteworthy, but the penning of the letter itself. So far as can be ascertained this is the first letter written in her own hand by a lady of rank in the English language rather than in the courtly French or Latin one would have expected.

John de Pelham was rewarded by the new king, Henry IV, with the constableship of Pevensey and the estates of the 'Honour of the Eagle' not merely for his own lifetime but as a legacy for all his male descendants. Male descendants, of course: a poor acknowledgement of the part played by the lady in the matter. One suspects that once the master was home the mistress of the castle ceased to have any say in its destinies and was expected to revert to the role of a gracefully feminine, loving, subservient wife. She must dress to please her husband, attend to his creature comforts, and tempt him with such perfumes and makeup as were available and allowable: much frowned on by the Church, the commonest makeup was a fine white flour used to lighten the complexion and, in all probability, cover the blemishes of commonplace illnesses and unbalanced diet.

In his absence, as in his presence, it was in order for her to listen to the songs of troubadours and verbose poems of courtly love – the medieval equivalent of the romantic novel and women's magazine serials – and to joke archly about them with her lord. But although a women might dabble with sentimental fantasies, and even have male acquaintances dancing attendance on her and pouring out conventional flowery phrases, it was all play-acting – and had best remain so. A man's adultery while away, or at home with the castle wenches and those in his fields and villages, was winked at; but a lady's adultery was a criminal blot on the escutcheon.

While the daughters of the family would, as we have seen, be sent away to other castles to be taught weaving, sewing, embroidery, cooking, social graces and household administration, the boys were sent from home for a tougher curriculum. In their infant years they had shared with their sisters the company of their mother and her attendants. By the age of eight or nine it was considered inadvisable that they should be pampered in exclusively feminine company, and so their training for knighthood began. Placed in the castle of a superior lord or with some influential uncle or cousin, a boy would be tutored in Latin and French and possibly a few other fitting subjects, but would devote most of his time to physical exercise and practical duties. He groomed horses, became a sort of batman to the knight or knights charged with his military tuition, learned the etiquette of the table, and waited on his lord. It was his duty, perhaps shared on a rota with other trainees, to help the master of the castle dress in the morning, comb his hair, and select his attire for the day. Strict rules governed the carving of meat and the presentation on bended knee of his lord's wine cup; and, indeed, everything else about behaviour at table:

> When you enter your lord's presence, say 'God speed' and humbly greet all present . . . Do not sit down until you are told to and keep your hands and feet still, not scratching yourself or leaning against a post. . . . Do not lean on the table and make a mess on the cloth or drink with a full mouth. Do not pick your nose, teeth or nails, or take so much that you cannot answer when anyone speaks to you.

By the time a lad was 14 he was expected to qualify as a competent squire, adept at fencing, hunting and hawking, horsemanship and tilting.

Each castle had its tiltyard or lists, a space between the main curtain wall and an outer crenellated wall above the moat. Here in time of peace the knights would keep in trim by riding with their lances against a wooden dummy known as a quintain, spinning on a post, or would try at speed to thrust the lance tip into a slot or dangling loop. The favourite competitive sport was jousting, when one knight in full array would try to unhorse another by skilful use of shield and lance – a sport which would be played in deadly earnest when the day for real battle came.

An attendant squire looked forward to the day when he, too, would be judged worthy to take part in such knightly bouts. When that time came he

34
A scene from the Luttrell Psalter showing the presentation of helmet and shield to Sir Geoffrey Luttrell by his wife and daughter-in-law.

35
A staircase in the keep of Pevensey castle.

braced himself for the initiation and, after a preliminary day of roistering with old friends, among them squires who now regarded him as a senior boy, began the solemn ritual.

The night before his induction he bathed and then donned fresh white garments and a red robe, and when the chaplain had blessed his sword – perhaps a gift from his father, with a holy relic enshrined in the pommel – he laid it on the chapel altar and stood or knelt in vigil through the hours of darkness, praying for the purification of his soul. At dawn the chaplain came to hear his confession and celebrate mass; and then the young acolyte would, attired in his finest shirt, tunic, shoes and hose, breakfast with his friends and members of his family who had ridden over for the ceremony.

A platform had been set up at one end of the lists. Minstrels played as the aspirant was ceremoniously attired by tutelary knights in helmet and armour, one of the most symbolic moments in the ritual being the girding on of spurs. The consecrated sword was brought from the altar, and its hilt kissed by the squire.

Today we have seen on film and television, or perhaps in some live ceremonial, the light accolade on head or shoulder with a sword blade. This is a relic of the much more forceful buffet bestowed long ago by the father or lord of a knight-to-be, or by one of his senior sponsors: no gently symbolic tap but an open-handed whack which often knocked the recipient sideways.

The dubbing accomplished, the new-made knight returned to the chapel and for a brief spell replaced his sword on the altar while he indulged in the attendant festivities.

36
A lady at her toilet.

37
Jousting in the lists, to a background of music and with one contestant being urged on by his lady love.

38
A Crusader in late 12th-century chain-mail armour and linen surcoat, waiting to receive his heavy helmet.

39
The dubbing of a knight.

40
An ivory representing a 'siege of the castle of love'.

He was now accepted as a member of the order of chivalry. This, based on an amalgam of ideals fashioned by imaginative pseudo-historians and troubadours, preached the virtues of disinterested bravery not only on the battlefield but in the aftermath of such strife; mercy to a conquered foe, courtesy and assistance to damsels in distress, a shunning of boastfulness, pride in one's honour but humility before God. War in itself was never denounced. 'Barons', exhorted the lyricist Bertrand de Born (forever damned by Dante for his jingoism), 'mortgage your castles, domains, cities, but never give up war.' And the chivalry which spared the vanquished made a distinction between those of knightly status and those of lower rank. The very word 'chivalry' identifies the chevalier or mounted gentleman-at-arms, as opposed to the common foot soldier and peasant. Noblemen played according to their own courtly rules but recognised no rules in their dealings with the lower orders. When Kenilworth was besieged in June 1266 and by October saw no sign of relief forces, the garrison commander negotiated a truce whereby it was agreed that if within 40 more days no help arrived he might surrender without loss of face. In mid December it became clear that the absent lord of the castle would bring no succour; whereupon the commander surrendered, and his entourage was treated with honour by the besiegers.

No such compassion had been shown to the blameless peasantry of the neighbourhood. Defenceless, the villein and serf were without legal, military or clerical protection. Their crops could be filched by defenders or attackers alike, their children ridden down, their homesteads demolished. The chivalrous leader of besieging forces might deliberately lay waste the countryside about his opponent's castle, bankrupt him by desolating his fields and orchards, and slaughter his labourers without that rival impugning for one moment his innate sense of honour. 'When two nobles quarrel, the poor man's thatch goes up in flames.'

Who in those days was truly poor: what, in medieval terms, was meant by poverty?

41
Bronze figure of a knight, late 13th or early 14th century.

CHAPTER III

The Demesne

Even when the dangers of rebellion, civil war, or petty conflict with some rival baron were at their lowest, so making it possible to relax military watchfulness, the inhabitants of a castle still led a fairly circumscribed life. If they went visiting they needed a cumbersome baggage train and a well-armed escort, and had to be confident of the castle constable's ability to mount an immediate defence if something went wrong while their backs were turned. And if they were not travelling and living on friends' hospitality but staying a while at home, there was the constant need for victualling from the forest and manors, especially when hospitality had to be repaid. The castle, though originally set up to intimidate a particular area of countryside, existed largely by what that countryside could bring it.

As well as their castle techniques the Normans had brought with them their own concept of the manor, comprising the lord's personal demesne and those related lands over whose tenants he exercised feudal rights and from whom he took payment in kind, labour, or money. A great baronial estate might include several distinct manors, some centred on one village, others embracing several villages and hamlets; and there were instances of villages being divided between two manors – making, one would think, for some difficulties in management and a great deal of conflict.

The manorial system ran in parallel with the military feudal system. Theoretically the lord of the castle would sustain his workers and protect their interests with his soldiers in return for their supplying him with food and the products of their rural workshops. In harsh fact he would protect them only when that suited *his* interests, and they could count on him far less than could the least of his men-at-arms.

The manorial fief was built around the demesne, the land which the lord had chosen for his own. In return for working two or three days a week throughout the year on these fields, and perhaps more intensively at certain times when called on, the peasant was granted a measure of land for himself: but even from that concession the lord would expect certain gifts of produce, especially on religious feast days, and the village priest also claimed a tenth share to be delivered to his tithe barn. If the lord's fields needed manuring he could order the village cattle or sheep to be grazed on them. If, on the other hand, he wished to graze his sheep on the peasants' land he availed himself of his right of 'fold course'. At sowing or harvest he could require a man's services at just the time when that man needed to tend his own plot to its best advantage. In due course those who had managed in spite of all exactions to build up relatively prosperous patches of farmland by selling surplus produce at market or to travelling merchants might commute their obligations into cash payments, a civil version of scutage; but even then up to half the fruits of their labour would still, one way and another, go into the lord's kitchens or his pocket.

These village labourers fell roughly into two categories. Some were classed as freemen; the others as villeins, holding the land by servile tenure.

Domesday Book records about one-eighth of the population, largely in the north and north-east, as freeholders with a customary right to manage their own land, sell it, and move away if so inclined. Even under Norman domination they retained this status provided they paid an agreed rent to the lord of the estate or an agreed quantity of produce at specified times

42
At work on the land: (a) scything; (b) threshing; (c) sheep in the pen.

each year. They could hire themselves out for wages if the lord needed extra help, but he could not demand this as he could from his other servile tenants. In case of a clash between a lord and these freemen they, again unlike the tied villeins, could appeal to the royal courts, though this was rarely done: a baron usually had enough influence to sway the king's justice against lesser mortals, however valid their claims.

Among the freemen could be found craftsmen such as smiths, thatchers, carpenters and shoemakers. The miller was perhaps the most privileged of all, paying a rent to the lord for the monopoly of his mill and charging the villagers – often overcharging – for grinding their corn.

In theory an unfree man might buy his freedom with money saved from his labours, but there was many a legal argument about this. Opponents of such transactions maintained that since all land and its fruits belonged to the lord, any profit made by one of the lord's serfs was the lord's profit, which ought not to be whittled away. Nevertheless a few men did manage to achieve enfranchisement by such payments; others by training as specialised craftsmen; and others, it may be, by marrying into the castle staff and somehow winning the lord's favour and his agreement to liberate them from their feudal caste.

Freedom did not necessarily mean social or financial superiority. Many a so-called freeholder, working a few acres of his own croft, was worse off than a villein with 30 acres, and frequently had to sell his services to such a villein. At least, though, he could choose how and where he should sell such services. The serf, no matter how snug, was tied to the land – and to a particular tract of that land. He could not sell his holding, his cottage, or his stock, without permission. Dispose of one animal and he must pay his lord a fee. Wishing to marry, he must seek his lord's approval and pay a fee. If one of his daughters wished to marry there would be a fine known as a

43
A sack of flour is collected from the manorial windmill. Villagers were compelled to use their lord's mill and pay a percentage of the resulting flour to him for the service, even when they might often have preferred to grind it by hand at home.

merchat. This was much higher if she married outside the community, thereby working and breeding for the benefit of another manor. At death there was a further duty, the heriot. Or, rather, there were two of these: the lord took the dead man's best beast, the priest his second-best as a 'soul scot' or mortuary. If there were no livestock to meet this claim, clothes or the best items of domestic equipment were taken. Just as no noble tenant's son could inherit without paying a 'relief' for the regrant, so the humblest bondsman could not continue to work his deceased father's land until death duties were paid.

The unfree man was bound to his lord and the rituals of the land by custom. That same body of accumulated custom could to a limited extent be used by the community against a misguided or insecure lord; but if he chose to be tyrannical he could usually get his own way. The real distinction between the free and the unfree has been summed up in the observation that the lord was under no legal liability, and felt himself under no moral obligation, to let any serf know the night before what tasks might be required of him in the morning.

Most sensible magnates did not enforce their rights too harshly. They needed villeins to work their land, and docile men worked better than the disaffected. There was no point in exacting the last second of a man's manorial service if there was no real need for him: on many an estate the two or three obligatory days a week would in reality be no more than a couple of half-days, or even one incomplete day, with a mutual agreement that all-out effort would be called for at sowing, harvest and other crucial times. It did the land and its crops little good if large numbers of the oppressed work force slacked on the job or even ran away. Not that many did run away, even in the most trying times: a villein was not free to seek employment elsewhere, and most runaways would be returned or recaptured within a short time, to be flogged and probably have tongue or ears chopped off.

Many pre-Norman customs and courts of shire and hundred remained, but superimposed on them were the feudal patterns of Norman administration. There was a manorial court to which tenants were summoned to settle all transfers of land, fines and taxes, and disputes. The verderers' court imposed penalties for those defying forest law. Many other felonies were dealt with at the hundred court. Often the various bodies overlapped. Within them the villein had no real standing. He might plead ancient custom and, if he were lucky, have this recognised, or might have some contentious point regarding outstanding debts or toll payments or field boundaries settled in his favour; but he could not assert anything as his right.

Twice a year there was a View of Frankpledge, a legacy of the Saxon procedure of appointing ten men, or a tithing, to be responsible for breaches of the peace within their neighbourhood. At first the hearings had been at the Sheriff's Tourn, but the lords soon took a personal interest because from such proceedings they realised they could derive a personal profit, and so the hearings were transferred to the manorial Court Leet. Here all petty misdeeds came up for judgement and usually the imposition of a fine which found its way into the lord's coffers. At such a meeting, also, the local constable, ale taster and other officials would be appointed or confirmed in office. Major transgressions were referred to the travelling royal courts.

*　　　*　　　*

Although the Normans wrought many changes in the social structure of the country, their coming had little effect on the English landscape other than the appearance of so many castles. Agriculture, which with the aid of the improved Belgic plough and its Roman successors had made great advances from the small enclosed fields of the Celts to the open fields of the Saxons, went on much the same as it had done under those Saxons. Local variations were conditioned by the lie of the land, its soil and natural resources, be they on hill, moorland or arable plain; but in general, without wishing to over-simplify, it may be said that peasants in most regions worked a conventional two-field or, increasingly, three-field system.

Each of three open spaces, bare of hedges, would be divided into sections each of ten acres known as a fardel, farthingale or furlong, from the optimum length of a furrow. These were communally ploughed with a team of oxen, both beasts and human labour being pooled for this, but within the fardel were sub-divisions of acre and half-acre allocated to individual farmers who did their own sowing and reaping. Distribution of these strips has puzzled many a student. A villein's quota of plots did not lie side by side but would be scattered all over the main fields, involving him in a lot of plodding to and fro and all too often in acrimonious disputes with neighbours over the exact boundary of a strip or over the damage caused by crossing or circumnavigating those neighbours' intervening strips. It may have been that each member of a group acquired additional slices of territory as the cultivable area was pushed out from its beginnings, and that these slices were shared out according to mutual agreement on position and fertility, with some allowance made for different family needs and the capabilities of different families.

In the three-field system, only two would be planted each year with crops agreed between the villagers, the third being left fallow to recuperate. A characteristic rotation would start with wheat and perhaps rye in Field 1; barley and oats, perhaps beans or peas, in Field 2; Field 3 lying fallow. Next year the wheat and rye would move into Field 3, the barley into Field 1, and Field 2 would be left fallow; and so on.

In a two-field system common in the uplands, crops and sheep

44
Shoeing a horse.

alternated. And there, as elsewhere, animals were whenever possible also grazed on common land. All members of the community were supposed to take part in clearing wasteland and, where royal or baronial permission had been granted, to carving fresh pastures out of woodland. The clearings made for swine pasture by early Saxon settlers, giving the ending -*den* to so many southern towns and villages, had in too many cases been swallowed up by forest law; but every opportunity was taken of making fresh clearings.

When a peasant could afford it he would buy permission to open up such entries into the woodland. If a royal forest were involved, this permission would have to come from the Crown. On a baronial estate the lord might welcome such signs of initiative and the extra income and foodstuffs which would result. Such clearings or enclosures along the edge of a wood or on rough scrubland were known as assarts, and the lessee was allowed to work them pretty much as he liked. Obviously methods of cultivation differed

45
Reaping under the watchful eye
of a supervisor.

46
Bringing home the game.

from those on open arable land. To avoid infringement of forest laws, such concessions were usually hedged and enclosed, and so had to be worked individually rather than communally. In spite of meaning extra labour for a man and his family they did thus confer a certain rare freedom on him.

Often a farmer would simply start work unobtrusively on such a patch without asking for permission and without laying out a penny. In scattered communities it might take some time before his operations attracted official attention; and then he would philosophically pay the fine, which as a general rule was converted into a regular rental rather than a fine. A few reckless souls even ventured to chisel little segments out of the edges of royal forests, and in court records there are reports of some going so far as to build huts within the sacred precincts. This was really asking for trouble.

Forest law weighed heavily on those trying to wrest a living from the soil. The sight of so much untilled land being reserved for the sport of a wealthy few must have been a constant irritation. In Devon a large consortium of farmers were determined enough, and solvent enough, to approach King John at one of the times when he was desperate for money and buy from him the right to disafforest the entire county save for Exmoor and Dartmoor. The price in modern terms ran to several hundred thousand pounds.

*   *   *

The peasant's house, with its patch of kitchen garden, was often only a mud or clunch hovel containing one room. When he and his family could add to it, or build something larger and more lasting, they still spent most of their time in one main room – a cramped miniature of the castle or manor hall where everything went on, only in this case the animals which shared it were not favourite hunting dogs and falcons but pigs, fowl and maybe a precious cow.

*47
A cruck building. Two curved
trunks or branches were driven
into the ground some feet apart
and then pulled together at the
top to form an arch, like a
couple of elephant tusks or
whalebone. When a sequence of
these had been set up one behind
another, a ridge pole was laid
along the top to link them, and
bracing timbers might be added
across the ends and along the
sides.*

If the lord of the manor was either a benevolent man or at least one
enlightened as to his own long-term interests, he would allow timber from
his estates for the construction of more lasting buildings. Nothing remains
today of those old huts walled with cob or clay clump, but we can still find
examples of early cruck cottages in the north, Midlands and west, especially
in Herefordshire. This introduction of timber trusses simplified and
strengthened every other feature of the building. Wattle-and-daub walls
were laid on the skeleton: twigs woven into a rough mesh supporting the
daub of straw, clay and dung. Roofs were usually thatched with straw or
reeds. In certain districts one of the duties imposed by the lord was the

cutting of reeds for this purpose; and, true to form, he was swift to ordain that if the labourer wished to dodge this duty there would have to be remission payment, in this case known as sedge silver.

Inside, the floor was of hard trampled earth. The fire burned on an open hearth, perhaps on a baked clay foundation or iron plate, with smoke escaping through the unglazed windows, through holes in the thatch, or under the eaves. Most cooking utensils were of wood or earthenware, with the occasional brass or iron skillet. The trestle table and wooden stools had been made, like the wooden platters and bowls, during winter evenings, and if there were space against the walls a few pallets might be set there to carry bedding: straw or flock mattresses, and home-woven blankets which could also serve as cloaks or saddle blankets. Personal belongings and best clothes, if any, were stored in a wooden chest.

Food was more monotonous than that provided in castle or manor hall. Whatever ingredients might be used, the texture was usually that of thin gruel devoid of any nourishing meat, perhaps filled out with beans and coarse corn, or a porridge of meal and milk. Many a meal consisted simply of a pot of ale and a hunk of bread, sometimes with cheese. Often the cottager would surely look forward to the busy time when he was required to work free for his lord until late in the day, for then it was usual for the lord to provide fairly generous food and drink.

Salted pork and bacon were the only flesh the villein could expect to see at all regularly – and not a great deal of that.

Clothing was nearly all made at home. Women had not merely to work in the fields beside their menfolk and cook for them and bear their children, but to spin their own wool, make linen from coarse hemp, and plait straw for animals' harness. An old song saw little that was idyllic in this rustic existence:

> A woman is a worthy wyght,
> She serveth a man both daye and nyght;
> Thereto she putteth all her might,
> And yet she hathe but care and woo.

48
A 14th-century bronze ewer, probably from Berkeley castle.

To wash clothes the women would go to the village stream and, using a cleansing solution of lye and clay or fuller's earth, pound the garments with wooden paddles. These had probably been made by the men, who also carved out wooden clogs for the family – better than the thick cloth shoes sometimes worn, which were a poor defence against rain and mud.

The castle damsel might lament her inability to marry the man of her choice, if she ever had the chance of an actual choice. And when wed, she had no choice but to tread the steps devised for her. The peasant girl had few conventions to observe and no dynastic ambitions to satisfy. Yet even here there must have been many marriages of convenience. A large family was useful in some ways: the demesne work could be shared out, leaving several permanently at home to work the family plots. But if the numbers grew too great for those acres to support, parents could hardly be blamed for nudging a marriageable daughter towards, say, the only son of a family which found it difficult to cope with its land.

Lord and priest collected their fees for the wedding; and it might be that the officiating priest was in fact a close relation of one of the young couple, perhaps even a brother.

*　　　*　　　*

The baron had his own chapel and his own chaplain. His manor had its parish church and parish priest, whose appointment depended on the lord's wishes, perhaps swayed by the influence of some powerful monastery which he himself had endowed. It has been estimated that in the Middle Ages there was a church for every 40 or 50 households in England. Tourists today often marvel at huge churches in situations where it seems there could never have been a congregation large enough to fill them. Was there a prosperous town which mysteriously vanished; or are countryfolk less devout today? The answer is that there rarely was such a congregation, even in those ages when regular attendance was virtually compulsory. Churches were built by rich lords and rich abbots not merely for the service of local worshippers but as an architectural affirmation of their own piety.

A religious house might supply some of the priests for churches and subsidiary chapels on baronial and manorial estates, and such appointees would pay a pension and other fees to the minster or mother church. The majority of appointments were made by private owners: every gentleman liked to control his own church and his own parson. Livings were created, donated, bought, or sold off. Tithes and fees were collected – great tithe for larger livestock and crops, lesser tithe for such smaller stock as hens and other minor items, imposts due at birth, marriage and death – and distributed according to the dictates of the owner. The resident cleric did not always get much of the tithe for himself: the abbot who had presented him with the living might take the larger part and graciously allow him a pittance; the lord who had built or bought the church would behave likewise; or an absentee rector who had installed him as vicar would similarly collect the tithe and decide what proportion, if any, to pass down.

In a prosperous and none too demanding a community the incumbent might be a younger son of the nobility, with a comfortable living in a spiritual sinecure. If he wished to absent himself from all real duties he could pay a wage to some lowlier cleric. The majority of priests came from humble backgrounds: sons of the peasantry, they were dedicated young to the service of the Church and, if accepted, had to raise a fee for their formal tonsuring. Little richer than their brothers, cousins and neighbours, they were given strips of land to work for themselves – their glebe land – and

49
The Norman church of Fingest in Buckinghamshire, with a double saddleback roof to its tower.

50
The Place Farm tithe barn at Tisbury, Wiltshire, a medieval thatched barn believed to be the largest of its kind in England. Here were delivered and stored the tithes due to near-by Shaftesbury abbey.

often found themselves in competition with their own flock and their own kith and kin. Generally illiterate, and with little skill in interpreting Holy Writ to their congregation or advising on spiritual matters, they were as often resented as respected. Some, whether of high or low origin, neglected all save their barest duties: one such is caricatured in Langland's *Piers the Plowman* as Sloth the Parson. Others put agriculture well before sanctity, grazing their animals in the churchyard, brewing ale within the church, and assiduously bargaining against their own parishioners at market.

But Chaucer has left us a testimony to another kind of priest, the kind who has always existed and of whom we prefer to think:

> Wyd was his parisshe, and houses fer asonder
> But he ne lafte nat for reyn ne thonder,
> In siknesse nor in meschief to visite
> The ferreste in his parrisshe, muche and lite

CHAPTER IV

UNWELCOME VISITORS

Why, it may be asked, should a chapter on unwelcome visitors precede one dealing with those who were welcome? It comes in this order because, as has been established, the castle was for many generations primarily a defence of a lord's life and privileges rather than a place of family intimacy and social relaxation. The owner and his sentries were always alert for an enemy on the horizon rather than a desirable guest.

Not that the lord was always at home when his enemy arrived. Visiting other estates, attending on the king or conspiring against the king, in times of unrest he was indeed most likely to be occupied elsewhere. Defence then had to be entrusted to the constable of the castle. Given fair warning, the defenders would appropriate as much food as possible from the immediate neighbourhood. Taken by surprise, they would have to ration out such stocks as were normally stored on the premises, much of them salted or smoked for preservation. The constable might also have to hire or conscript makeshift defenders if the lord had taken away with him a substantial proportion of those who owed him knight-service.

In open battle, mounted knights were of paramount importance. Few foot soldiers could withstand a cavalry charge. A trained archer or daring pikeman might bring down a horse and with it the heavily clad knight, who was then at a disadvantage; but they were just as likely to be trampled down in the attempt.

Bowmen could, in the right conditions and especially on terrain too steep or uneven for horsemen to operate at their best, play a crucial part in the outcome of a battle, sometimes virtually deciding it before any final hand-to-hand struggle could begin. And once an engagement had been broken off so that the defenders could flee to refuge within their fortifications, the archer became of more importance than the knight: no castle could ever be taken by a cavalry charge.

In the twelfth century there were two fresh developments in the bow. Short bows such as those used at the battle of Hastings were still in use, but now the powerful arbalest or crossbow was devised. A bow of steel or laminated wood was fastened into a crosswise wooden stock. Its bowstring was cranked back by a handle and retained in a notch until ready to be

51
A scene from the Bury Bible.

triggered off. The short bolt, or quarrel, which this fired wrought such damage that there were ecclesiastical protests about its use – it was specifically condemned by the Lateran Council in 1139 – and even those lords who hired crossbowmen were uneasy. In the time of King John many of these hirelings were in fact foreign mercenaries, which added to the loathing felt for the weapon by most chivalrous (if chauvinistic) combatants.

Moral issues rarely play any great part in war, however, and the crossbow's decline in importance was due more to its slowness of operation. It was overtaken by the second and more significant invention of the century. This was the longbow, six feet in length and firing a shaft three feet long which took its name, a 'cloth-yard', from the standard measurement of a yard of cloth. It appears to have been a Welsh invention, acquired by Edward I during his campaigns in Wales and later used in major battles against the Scots and the French, most famously at Crécy and Agincourt. Its ability to fire four or five shafts in the time it took a crossbowman to re-load for one shot put it in the forefront of archers' weapons; and for centuries to come all young men in the country were ordered to practise regularly at the butts, and special legislation covered the growing and felling of yew trees, providers of the finest bows.

Once a conflict in the field had changed into the siege of a castle, however, the crossbowman still had his uses. His bolts travelled faster than the arrows of the longbow and had much greater powers of penetration. Some siege engines, in fact, were no more than murderously expanded versions of a crossbow.

52
A French depiction of the battle of Crécy showing a confrontation of crossbows and longbows and making it clear how much time could be fatally lost in loading and cranking up the crossbow.

A prolonged siege was a dreary business for both sides, and frustrating when the pace of some royal or inter-baronial campaign demanded a quick decision. Before settling down to starve out the garrison – devastating the fields, crops and homes of the local peasantry in the process – the attackers would bring up all their aggressive resources to force a breach in the outer walls and ultimately into the inner stronghold. Siege machinery improved as the years went by. In reply, the construction of castles grew more complex. Throughout history every defence has provoked more sophisticated assault weaponry, which in turn is met by a further improvement in defences, and so on until we reach the present insanity of ballistic missiles and anti-ballistic missiles and anti-anti-ballistic missiles.

53
An arrow slit in one of the outer wall towers of Caerphilly castle.

The motte-and-bailey fort had long ceased to be an adequate protection save in small localised skirmishes. The keep, with its thick walls and tiny windows through which it was difficult for an attacker to aim any effective shot but through which defenders could fire down on the enemy, presented a more formidable problem. But if the assailants could get close enough, even the greatest tower or sturdiest wall bastion was in real danger from sappers chipping away corners of masonry or undermining the foundations.

A first defensive measure then, was to keep these demolition experts at a distance, picking them off every time they tried to dash for stretches of the walls against which shooting from above was difficult.

Where possible, water was utilised as one of the most effective barriers. The great lakes of Caerphilly and Kenilworth made direct assault almost impossible. Even an ordinary moat was a major deterrent: once the

54
Caerphilly castle, showing the complex water defences and, in the left-hand corner of the main buildings, the drum tower leaning outwards after an attempt to destroy it during the Civil War.

drawbridge was up, the water had to be crossed by an extemporised causeway of earth, stones and even dead bodies – of which there would be no shortage, exposed as the attackers were during the entire operation to a hail of missiles from the battlements. Before even starting such a tricky job it was necessary to bring up, or construct on the spot, some sort of cover. These portable shelters, or 'tortoises', were pushed forward over the bridge-builders' heads. Sides and roofing usually consisted of raw hides, or metal plates if they could be brought up in time. Wood was not recommended: the defenders would be only too happy to pour down upon it fire fed with bacon or grease.

The attackers themselves employed fire against any vulnerable part of the defences. Gates and wooden stockades of earlier mottes and baileys had proved especially vulnerable. Stone castles were not so easy to set alight but there was always the chance of firing the drawbridge, drawn up into its gatehouse, and with the right sort of mechanical catapult it was possible to hurl fire over the battlements into the courts and inner buildings. The most dreaded was 'Greek fire', a mixture of naphtha, sulphur and quicklime which ignited spontaneously when moistened, and blazed fiercely.

If a causeway was successfully built across the moat, or if the castle had only a dry moat which could be crossed dry-shod in spite of the dangers of the steep, exposed approach to the lower courses of the curtain wall, then siege engines would be trundled forward to batter against the stonework, while sappers endeavoured to bring down a sizeable chunk of that stonework. The painstaking approach to this task was epitomised in the use of the bore or 'mouse', an iron gouge which nibbled away around one stone at a time until the fabric was loosened and then picks could be used to remove larger segments.

Safer from the attentions of the defenders, and more spectacular if it worked, was an attack on the foundations through a tunnel. Driving a passage through dangerously unstable earth, the sappers used timbers to prop up the roof in just the way they were to be used in the First World War. When they reached the target area the tunnel was packed with branches, brushwood, rags, grease – anything which would burn – and the whole mass set ablaze. The sappers retired as speedily as miners always do when a charge has been fired. If all went well, the timbers burnt through and collapsed, and into the weakened earth collapsed also a wall tower or a corner of the keep itself. Once such a breach had been made, the assault forces were concentrated there.

The only possible counter-attack, and a very risky one, was the digging of a tunnel from inside, aimed at breaking into the underground invasion route. This could be done only when careful observation had identified the line of approach; and it led to some cramped fighting in the most claustrophobic conditions.

It was against such erosion of sharp corners and angles that the circular keep and bastion were conceived. With them, sheer brute force above ground level was all that counted – all, that is, save for the patience in the long run to let the human frame within collapse from lack of food and water, if the stone frame refused to yield.

The more aggressive siege engines derived from the principle of the catapult or that of the magnified crossbow. There were fundamentally two methods of assault: throwing things *over* the walls, and throwing things *at* them. Rocks, scrap metal and fire were hurled over the defences; and there was a pleasant custom of tossing the reeking, decaying corpses of long-dead horses in the hope of starting up an epidemic of some contagious or infectious disease. Range, direction and elevation . . . the relevant factors are little changed, even when the propulsive power has become that of the rocket. Flame-throwers are not new. And the predecessors of the tanks of our day were the head-on assault machines which threw themselves repeatedly at the walls.

Among the throwing devices known in general as *petrariae* because stone was the main ammunition were the mangonel, the trebuchet, the ballista or springald, and the outsize arbalest. The arbalest and ballista fired metal bolts or stones – the crossbow, large or small, being in effect a development of the ballista known in Roman times. These larger missile dischargers worked on the principle of torsion, with stretched cords and thongs launching reasonably well aimed projectiles at bowmen and other defenders on the battlements.

The mangonel employed a similar principle. Twisted cords were

55
(a) A trebuchet. The throwing arm was pivoted on an upright, with weights at one end and a sling for the missile at the other. The longer end was pulled down, the sling filled, and after release the effect was that of an unevenly balanced seesaw: the heavy end smacked violently down, while the occupant of the other end soared in a high trajectory finishing in or over the defending wall.
(b) This representation of Saul attacking the Ammonites is conceived in 13th-century terms and includes the loading of a siege engine which seems to be a cross between a trebuchet and a mangonel.

tightened between two wooden uprights, the turn of the twist being towards the target. An arm with a ladle-shaped container was pulled down against the torsion of these strands, and a jagged rock or lump of metal loaded into it. When the loaded end was released, the swiftly slackening skein thudded the shaft of the 'ladle' against a cross-bar and released the projectile at high speed. The word 'gun' possibly derives from the middle syllable of 'mangonel'.

Another engine, the trebuchet, used counterweights to provide the necessary thrust.

Even when defences had been softened up by such devices, the actual seizure of the castle was still no foregone conclusion. It might be difficult to get enough men through a breach fast enough for them to be effective inside. Flanking fire from projecting towers in the wall would cut down attackers, and often an outward-slanting plinth at the base not merely made the last few feet awkward to scramble over but bounced back stones from above at unpredictable angles.

Now a 'tortoise' might serve another purpose, being rammed against a breach in the wall to cover the storming party. There were larger protected assault engines, too: tall mobile towers, roofed in to shield several floors of archers and men-at-arms, which would be pushed against the wall. If it were high enough it could lower its own drawbridge on to the battlements to disgorge its troops, while on the lowest floor sappers worked to start further breaches in the wall. Many of these erections acquired nicknames from the men who operated them or were threatened by them: the belfry, the bear, and the cat (though this last seems to have been interchangeable as a name for the smaller tortoise).

Some form of cover was also necessary when a battering ram was used. The ram, crude but effective if one could get a straight run at a gateway or an already weakened corner, was made from what material came to hand – the largest tree trunk available, fitted with a sharpened iron snout, to be swung repeatedly against its target or mounted on wheels and pushed forward by men under a wooden canopy.

At all times the attackers would be exposed to a hail of arrows, stones and filth from above. Behind the tops of walls and towers were parapets manned by archers who discharged their arrows down through the gaps between the square teeth of the crenellations. A further measure was the provision of machicolation around the heights of towers and gatehouses. Here a projecting parapet, sheltered by a wooden or stone wall, was provided with slats in its floor so that a variety of noxious liquids could be poured through the gaps between its supporting corbels upon those below. Also, if a ram were exposed, defenders above the threatened spot might lower looped ropes or some other kind of grapple to snare the iron-shod head and lessen or prevent its blow.

The most risky but, over the centuries, most common way of forcing entry into a castle was by means of long scaling ladders. Casualties were high. Unless there were a great many ladders and the ascent was pressed home frantically, defenders could push the tops out and away from the wall, shoot climbers off the rungs, or pick them off one at a time as they reached the battlements. But when the besiegers had neither materials nor time to construct heavy siege engines and belfries on the spot, the rate of casualties was something which had to be tactically appraised and ventured.

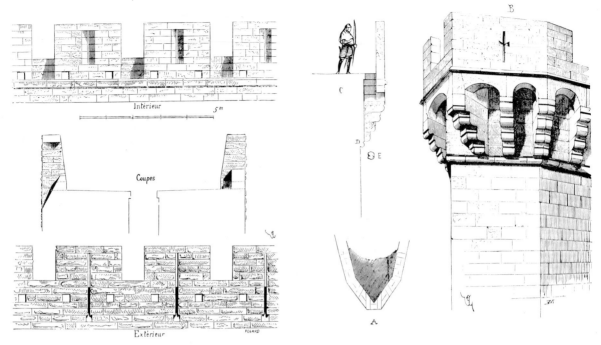

Intérieur

Coupes

Extérieur

PLGARD

57
Crenellation seen from within and from without. These battlements consisted of solid sections known as merlons, interspersed with gaps or crenels. Defenders could fire from the main embrasures or through arrow slits in the 'teeth'. Licence to crenellate – that is, to fortify one's home – was a royal favour bestowed only on trusted subjects.

58
Machicolation: two views, showing the openings between corbels through which burning materials or boiling liquid could be poured on the heads of attackers.

Attackers who managed to establish themselves on one section of the parapet could still not be sure of their grip on the rest. At intervals along the ledge were, as a rule, wooden sections which could be swiftly knocked out by retreating defenders, leaving the intruders perched in an unpleasantly exposed position. One can get a good idea of the situation by crossing one of the wooden bridges inserted to cover gaps in the surviving wall walkway of Framlingham castle.

When successive attacks had been thrown back and the enemy had withdrawn for a breathing space, there was still no great comfort for the defenders. Forces beleaguering the castle could bring up reinforcements and supplies. Those within might have heavy walls to protect them and military facilities to stave off the next attack, and the one after that; but lack of food and the worsening conditions in their living quarters would weaken them in the end. Once a castle had been surrounded, a successful break-out was rare. You sat and waited for relief to arrive; and that would depend on the fortunes of war elsewhere, of which it was hard to get news.

One of the worst aspects of a siege was confinement to that last stronghold in so many fortresses, the keep. Too many people and probably a large number of animals were crowded into the foul, smoky, restricted space for weeks on end. The interior was dark and depressing. If the windows had been large enough to let in plenty of light they would also have been large enough to let in arrows and other things. The latrines stank: nobody could venture to the base of the outside shaft to clean them. The food began to stink. So, in all probability, did the occupants, since water would be strictly rationed for drinking purposes only. With luck the water might hold out: the siting of a keep always took into account the incorporation of a reliable well. On the other hand it might not. Attackers frequently found ways of poisoning a well, often by tapping the spring which supplied it. Or, with so many people drawing from it, its supply might prove inadequate. Rochester surrendered to William Rufus in 1088 because internal conditions had become intolerable. Stephen's capture of Exeter castle was largely due to the sudden drying up of both its wells.

By the time of King John the defences of Rochester were much improved, and its defenders in 1215 of sterner stuff. Even after nearly two months, with their diet reduced to horseflesh and water, rebel forces still held out against a siege which the king himself supervised from start to finish. He was bent on digging the rebels out rather than starving them out. Ordering large supplies of picks, he put his men to chipping and smashing away at the bailey, and ultimately broke through. The next predictable move was the defenders' flight into the huge keep, 125 feet high. After a number of fruitless assaults John sent an order to his justiciar – the regent who attended to all matters of state in the king's absence – for supplies to fire a mine:

59
Hand-to-hand combat on scaling ladders.

> We command you that with all haste, by day and night, you send to us 40 bacon pigs of the fattest and those less good for eating to bring fire under the tower.

The shaft was driven, the props and brushwood steeped in fat and ignited, and the corner of the tower came down as planned.

Inside, the jubilant attackers found their task was still not ended. The keep was so huge that the flooring and roofing of the conventional great hall would not have been practicable, and a spine wall had been set across the building as a reinforcement. Regrouping behind this division, the defenders continued to resist until the royal forces finally overwhelmed them. The subduing of the castle had taken from early October until the last day of November.

But the keep was on its way out. Built to last, it remained stolid and uncompromising on its chosen sites; but played a less and less important part in the new styles of fortification which grew up around it or were established in new locations. There were better ways of keeping an enemy at bay than by simply shutting oneself away inside a bleak stone box.

Edward I's determination to hammer obedience into the Welsh and the Scots went hand in hand with an important development in castle building. The proven advantages of cylindrical bastions and gatehouses were incorporated in, and to some extent inspired, the most characteristic design of the thirteenth century – the concentric castle.

The basic technique was the construction of defensive walls one within

60
*Parapets along the walls of (a)
Caernarvon, showing
crenellations and arrow slits,
and (b) Framlingham, Suffolk,
its 12th-century shell
embellished with Tudor
chimneys.*

the other, so that an invader had more than one court or bailey to
conquer before he could move on to the innermost stronghold. The single
curtain wall enclosing a bailey had undoubtedly been strengthened by the
introduction of flanking towers from which defenders could fire along the
sweep of wall at their assailants; but the whole bailey was endangered if
even one of those towers was captured, and it was the captors' turn to
command the whole length of wall, inside as well as out. Now, with these
new methods, an outer wall was installed, preferably with curved bastions
at the corners, and a parapet behind the usual crenellations. Within was a
bailey, and behind that another, higher wall, so that if the outer defences
were taken the bowmen on the second line of defence could command the
lower wall and the space between. There were even examples of three
concentric walls with flanking towers. The keep, if one existed, was now
only one of many substantial, well defined buildings.

     To make things yet more difficult for soldiers who succeeded in

61
*The surviving keep of Rochester
castle on the river Medway in
Kent is the same as that which
King John besieged, save for the
replacement by a round corner
turret of the original square
turret successfully brought down
by his sappers.*

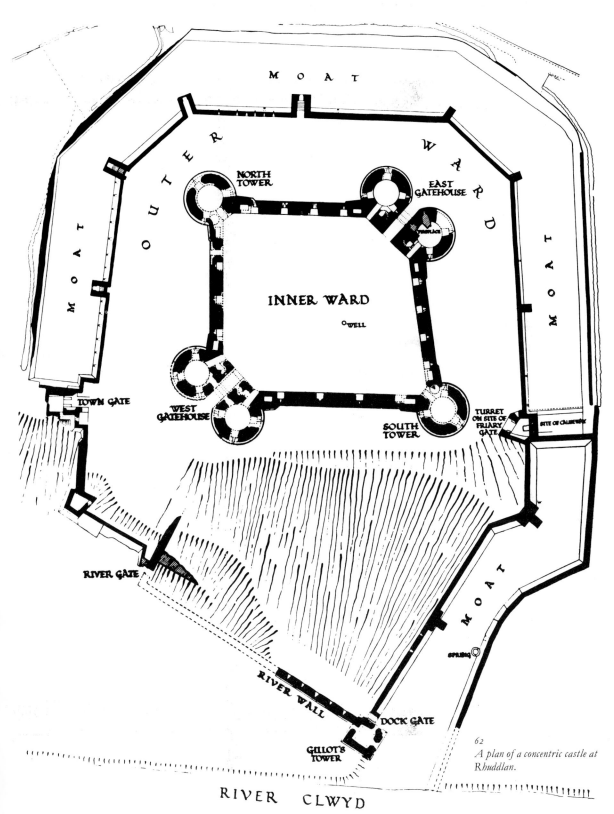

MOAT

OUTER WARD

MOAT

MOAT

NORTH TOWER

EAST GATEHOUSE

FIREPLACE

INNER WARD

o WELL

TOWN GATE

WEST GATEHOUSE

SOUTH TOWER

TURRET ON SITE OF FRIARY GATE

SITE OF CAUSEWAY

RIVER GATE

MOAT

SPRING o

RIVER WALL

DOCK GATE

GILLOT'S TOWER

62

A plan of a concentric castle at Rhuddlan.

RIVER CLWYD

63
Concentric castles set up by
Edward I at (a) Harlech, and
(b) Beaumaris.

breaching one or even two of the walls, the gateways were staggered. The outer one might enter from the south, while to assault the second one it was necessary to get round the bailey to an eastern gate in the second wall. If a third wall remained, its entrance might be yet further round on the north. At Caernarvon, its pattern of massive curtain walls and towers conditioned by the lie of the land rather than by abstract theory, access was made difficult by a sequence of gates and portcullises between one drawbridge and another set at a tight angle.

Edward I ordained the building of eight castles deep into Wales and on to its western coasts, many of them inspired by the new concentric model, as at Beaumaris, Harlech, and Rhuddlan. And while he thus set his royal mark upon Wales, his lords had been devising similar fortresses for themselves at places such as Kidwelly and Caerphilly, the latter reinforced with a complex of barbicans, lakes and a moat.

*   *   *

Whatever the architectural or dynastic changes, some sites remained important throughout the Middle Ages, and William I's original strategic network was reinforced rather than unpicked and refashioned. By the time of Edward I there had been great consolidation of the country, and judicial reform had alleviated many of the injustices of feudalism, at the same time reducing the capabilities of contentious barons to stir up national or local strife. But along the fringes there were still the old threats from French, Welsh and Scots.

William had strengthened the south coast and its hinterland and then imposed his wardens upon East Anglia, the south-west, the Midlands and Pennines, and along the western and northern borders. The closer to these borders and the farther from the heart of the kingdom, the more harassed the castellan.

Colchester, one of William's royal castles, was built in stone from the start, appropriating the Roman remains there and so providing a distinctive appearance with its mixture of rubble and ancient red tiles all mortared in together. Its keep is the larger of the only two known from the eleventh century, the other being the smaller Tower of London. In Norman hands and later, Colchester suffered less than in its previous history, when first the Romans seized it from the Catuvellauni and then the Iceni under Boudicca slaughtered the Roman inhabitants and their

64
Colchester, Essex.

supporters and plundered the city. Too sturdy in its Norman reincarnation to be easily taken, Colchester's fortress stood four-square as guardian of supply lines to the east coast and into Essex, Suffolk and Norfolk. Symbolically, even as late as 1648 it was Royalist at heart, and was besieged by Cromwell's troops until the town's two commanders surrendered and were executed as rebels.

Need for a royal watchdog in this region was several times emphasised by the outbursts of the unruly Bigod family. Granted 100 estates by William I, they built castles at Framlingham and Bungay, remained loyal to Henry I, backed Stephen and then turned him against, vowed allegiance to Henry II and then supported his unfilial sons, quarrelled with King John, and throughout several generations veered between feud and reconciliation, humble submission and arrogant defiance. In 1174, fleeing from Henry II across Essex through Suffolk, Hugh Bigod boasted:

> Now that I'm in my castle at Bungay
> Upon the river of Waveney,
> I will ne care for the King of Cockney.

In the end, though, he was forced to dismantle both Bungay and Framlingham. Later they were rebuilt, but then there were the quarrels with King John, and a later Roger Bigod who inherited Chepstow far to the west and became Earl Marshal of England under Henry III showed true to form by joining Simon de Montfort, deserting him for the king, and then passing the inheritance to a nephew who turned once more against the Crown.

Another royal castle in East Anglia, watching over the northern hump of the region, was that at Norwich. This was set up soon after the Conquest. Its imposing keep, added on a massive mound in the twelfth century, was faced with Caen stone and possibly some local flint. There were advantages to living in such a castle or within its 'fee'. Like Colchester it was no isolated outpost but a town dwelling, in this case existing more to dominate the town itself than to guard against hypothetical raids. Its staff could enjoy the sociable pleasures of the streets and markets and alehouses with few restrictions: anyone with a house inside the castle boundary was subject, in case of misdemeanour or more serious crime, not to the town justices but to trial by his fellow tenants within. This probably did not endear such tenants to those without the pale, oppressed as they might feel themselves by the castle's authoritarian shadow. In return for such privileges the insider was expected to rally to the defence of the castle if it were threatened.

West of Norwich we meet once more that Albini who married Henry I's widow and became lord of Arundel. During Stephen's reign he built a fortified home at Castle Rising with a keep similar in style to that at Norwich, and seems to have been able to keep it in the family through the turmoil of that period, despite being a supporter of Matilda. After Edward

65
Castle Rising, Norfolk.

III had executed Mortimer, his mother's lover and the prime mover behind
Edward II's murder in Berkeley castle, his mother Isabella was sent to
Castle Rising and lived out most of her remaining 30 years there. Legend
has it that she went mad with loneliness and that her ghostly screams can
still be heard echoing from the keep at night; but in sober fact her son
Edward and her grandson, the Black Prince, are known to have visited her
more than once, and she was allowed to make visits of her own – under
wary supervision – to friends in other parts of the land.

At Arundel we followed the fortunes of the Albinis and others in that
particular stronghold. Similar narratives could be recited of many a lordly
establishment on many a different site, with any number of them suffering
far stormier existences and far more dramatic incidents during sieges,
investments, demolitions and escapes.

A few days before the battle of Evesham, word reached Henry III's son
Edward that young Simon de Montfort intended to take some companions
from the Kenilworth garrison into town for an evening's entertainment
and a visit to the baths. The prince waited until most of the revellers were
drowsy, then set his men upon them. A number were rounded up, while
others made a dash for the castle. Young Simon had evidently been
intending to make a night of it, since it is recorded that he was still in his
nightshirt, in which he swam the castle lake to safety – a safety which, after
his father's defeat and death, did not last long.

Castles erected to counter local insurgents and Scottish raiders grow
thick on the ground from Pickering and Richmond northwards, forming a
broad defensive belt from Kendal and Carlisle in the west towards Barnard
Castle and Durham, and clustering ever more thickly in the vales of the Aln

66
A first-floor gallery in Castle Rising.

and the Coquet. Beside and beyond Hadrian's Wall even the parsonages were fortified, and pele towers jutted up from the landscape like miniature keeps.

The story of Durham is the story of its bishops, from the time when William granted the castle as an ecclesiastical fief on the understanding that its owners would fight the good fight in every sense. Alnwick, home of the great Percy family of Northumberland from the beginning of the fourteenth century, was half destroyed in border warfare and not restored until the late eighteenth century; but their castle at Warkworth, birthplace of Harry Hotspur, survived as a key fortress for more than 400 years. The major Norman fortress in Harbottle, however, is now only a jagged relic surrounded by its little village and by fields still with some furrow traces of Norman ploughing.

Dunstanburgh, built on the east coast in the early fourteenth century, changed hands four times during the Wars of the Roses, and has one colourful story to itself: trapped within during one of the sieges, Henry VI's wife, the forceful Margaret of Anjou, escaped by being let down from the tower to a waiting boat.

Of all coastal fortresses, Bamburgh is surely one of the most strategically important and has therefore had the most troublesome history. Even before the Normans came it was a site of great importance. On its rocky eminence, protected on one side by the sea, it was the royal city of Saxon kings of Northumbria from the sixth century on. First surrounded by a palisade and then by a wall, it was a combination of castle and fortified township. In 651 Penda of Mercia laid siege to it but, unable to breach the defences, decided to make a vast funeral pyre of it. Bede relates:

> Demolishing all the neighbouring villages, he carried to Bamburgh an immense quantity of wood and thatch, piling it high against the city wall on the landward side. Now, while all this was going on, the most reverend bishop Aidan was living on Farne Island, which lies nearly two miles from the city . . . and when the saint saw the column of smoke and flame rising above the city walls it is said he raised his eyes and hands to heaven, crying with grief: 'Lord, see what evil Penda is doing!' No sooner had he spoken than the wind shifted away from the city, and drove back the flames on to those who had kindled them, so wounding and unnerving them that they abandoned their attack on a city so clearly under the protection of God.

Other assaults on the citadel proved equally fruitless until the Danes came and, on two occasions, stormed and pillaged it.

Among those who endeavoured to dethrone William Rufus was the earl of Northumbria, who took refuge in Bamburgh only to be besieged by land and blockaded from the sea. Slipping out of the castle in the hope of summoning relief, he fell into the hands of the king's troops, but his wife

67
*Bamburgh, capital of the first
kings of Northumbria.*

continued the defence of the castle until the besiegers brought the earl
below the castle walls and threatened to blind him there and then if it were
not surrendered. His lady yielded.

In Stephen's time the castle held out for Matilda; and then was taken.
Henry II added the square keep in 1170, and thereafter Bamburgh played its
part in a succession of border conflicts and, in due course, in the Wars of
the Roses, when in spite of its apparently impregnable position it changed
hands several times. The real end came, for this medieval stronghold as for
many others, with the use of cannon and gunpowder against it. Besieged
after the battle of Hexham in 1464, it is believed to have been the first
English castle to be subdued by gunfire.

The blow was almost mortal. Bamburgh was abandoned until the
eighteenth century, restored, and then repaired more extensively and to
some extent reshaped at the end of the nineteenth. By then it had
abandoned all pretence to being a fortress, and in our own century has been
largely converted into flats, containing in fact more private accommodation than any castle in England apart from Windsor. Parts of it are
open to the public between Easter and September – which in a way
indicates that, in spite of its large armoury and weapon collection, what
remains of the original so frequently contested stronghold now belongs
more appropriately in a chapter on welcome visitors than in one on the
unwelcome kind.

CHAPTER V

WELCOME VISITORS

In both peace and war a medieval king spent more time on the move than sitting at home in his capital. It was not until the time of Henry II that the Exchequer was lodged in permanent headquarters at Westminster, with the royal justiciar taking charge in the king's absences, and not until that of Edward III that the Chancery also settled there. These absences were essential if a monarch was to maintain control of his scattered estates and barons, ensure the strict administration of justice through his courts, and in those days of slow and unreliable communications appraise personally the temper and troubles of his subjects.

When the king set out on his travels virtually his whole court went with him: personal retainers, armed guards, chancellor and chamberlain and constable, stewards, marshals, mounted knights and men at arms. Clerks of the wardrobe transported and guarded the king's valuables, documents and royal attire. In due course each royal residence and most other places he was likely to visit would be provided with a store cupboard beside the king's bedroom for these items, which in time took on the name of wardrobe in our modern sense. A chaplain accompanied the king, and his clerk was responsible for looking after vestments and vessels for the mass and perhaps a portable altar and a number of reliquaries. There were also hornblowers, huntsmen and keepers of the royal hounds – for one of the king's main relaxations while on tour was hunting in the various forests under his sway or in the care of his lords.

A great caravan of waggons carried royal furniture, clothing and valuables, and refreshments for when they should halt by the wayside. On the whole, though, most such refreshment was provided in the royal or baronial castles where they stayed two or three nights, or which for a longer period might serve as centre for official functions in the locality: assize courts, bestowal of knighthoods and other favours, and discussion of local defence and local loyalties with his higher tenants.

King John was rarely a month in any one place; and Walter Map's *De Nugis Curialium*, translated by M. R. James as *Concerning Courtiers' Trifles*, gives a rueful picture of the peripatetic Henry II:

68
A lady and her retinue are welcomed at a fortified town gate.

He was always on the move, travelling in unbearably long stages, like a post, and in this respect merciless beyond measure to the household that accompanied him: a great connoisseur of hounds and hawks, and most greedy of that vain sport: perpetually wakeful and at work.

Edward I is recorded as changing his abode three times a fortnight.

The great magnates with whom the king lodged were, of course, effusive in their expressions of the joy that his presence would bring them. After all, they owed him their domains and titles and must show suitable gratitude. But in private they probably lamented the impending arrival of the company and its baggage train. The cost of lodging and feeding the huge retinue, and entertaining the monarch in the style to which he was accustomed, must have been a serious burden on the lord, his tenants and his sub-tenants. Vast quantities of food had to be requisitioned from the countryside well in advance, stripping the barns and larders of knight, cottar and villein alike. It was not uncommon for the length of the royal

69
Provision carts with weapons and cooking pots hung from the sides.

stay to be conditioned by the supply of food and wine available. Once it had all run out, the king and his train would be on their way again like a plague of locusts seeking fresh harvests.

Before each move a reconnaissance party would be sent on ahead. It was their duty to ensure that the next resting-place was comfortably equipped and could guarantee to be suitably provisioned by the time the king arrived. A royal marshal scoured the district within a wide radius to track down and summarily imprison malcontents who might will mischief to the king. As with any such body of travellers, there were the usual camp followers: beggars snatching at crusts, petty confidence tricksters and prostitutes. Bolder harlots might be found within dark corners of a castle itself and had to be chased out, often to the regret of the lower ranks. If one was so venturesome as to continue her attempts, perhaps encouraged by a number of sex-starved archers or grooms, she was liable on capture to have her upper lip cut off.

To the mobile courts of justice would be brought at an appointed time any prisoners the sheriff wished to submit to the judgement of the king and his chancellor. Petitioners of many kinds took the opportunity of approaching their monarch – some of them, daringly, seeking royal justice over the heads of their manorial court which they fancied had wronged them.

The routine was much the same, though on a less regal scale, when a great magnate also went on tour of his estates. In travelling between those which were widely scattered, he would have to seek the hospitality of one of his peers. For example, Henry de Ferrers, forebear of the earls of Derby, possessed more than 200 estates: over 100 in Derbyshire, the rest distributed through 13 other counties. There was method behind the royal grants of such widely separated holdings. It was difficult for even the most cunning baron, if he were minded to treachery, to bring all his resources together for an attack on his sovereign lord. Some lords summoned their tenants to a central baronial court at regular intervals, which involved those tenants in a great deal of travelling and a loss of time, money and productive work. But most found that for part of the year they, too, must travel in order to keep proper surveillance over their fragmented properties.

Such a visitor was usually genuinely welcome at another lord's castle, provided the two were not involved in a private war at the time. Too large a retinue posed the same problems as the king's; but a lord or knight travelling comparatively light provided diversion from the drab routine and isolation of ordinary castle life. As castles and manor houses grew more civilised, one of the first additions was a guest room or even a whole range of lodgings.

After a day of legal business by the king or travelling magnate came the inevitable feasting in the great hall. A king often had a jester, a troubadour, or even a complete group of full-time musicians in his travelling entourage; but might relish the change provided by those hired for the occasion by his host.

And then there were the wandering minstrels and tumblers and others.

A band of strolling players was nearly always welcome at the castle. Like visiting knights errant, they had fresh tales to tell and new songs to enliven the gloomy interior. To be sure of their reception they would usually line up below the battlements and sing a chorus, awaiting the invitation to

70
A jester, with characteristic cap and bells.

71
King John I of Portugal entertaining John of Gaunt: a miniature from a Flemish illuminated manuscript executed for Edward IV in the late 15th century.

enter. If the hall had a minstrels' gallery they would be sent up there to sing and play. If not, they grouped at the end of the hall and started proceedings with another chorus or perhaps a purely instrumental piece.

Among the stringed instruments were those which one plucked, such as lutes and small harps, the gittern or guitar, and those which were bowed, such as the rebec and vièle, early members of the viol family. Wind instruments included flutes and pipes, possibly a horn or clarion – a high-pitched trumpet – and bagpipes. In the early Middle Ages the players, like singers, would perform one at a time or in unison: it took time for the beauties of polyphony and harmony to be explored.

Singers specialised for many decades in romantic themes often adapted from the lays of the French troubadours into English terms, making much of the gallantry of knight errants and bringing in King Arthur wherever possible. Such lyrics grew more and more sentimental as time went on, and more and more elaborate, until the audience's taste for them began to wane. Then, in place of the old tales of love and battle, singers turned to lighter ballads and more sophisticated love stories. All in all there were fewer martial ditties than one might suppose: wars in France were a royal affair, scarcely heard of in most parts of the homeland until belated news of a

defeat or victory arrived; and local rivalries were best not set to music.

While in the neighbourhood the itinerant musicians would try to increase their income by performing also for villagers or townsfolk. For this, it need hardly be said, they had to pay a fee to the local lord or, in a town, to some influential burgess who had leased the concession from his overlord. As well as making a collection, the performers could count on being fed and sometimes on receiving gifts of clothing to help them on their way.

If within the castle walls they had found it expedient to stick to songs of chivalry and legends of the past, many of them risked using more contemporary material among the labouring classes. Out in the countryside it was common for satirists to produce songs of what we would now call social significance. A popular song of its day was the source of John Ball's appeal for a peasant rebellion:

> When Adam delved and Eve span,
> Who was then the gentleman?

Many of the subversive stories which grew up around the name of Robin Hood were the fruit of the minstrels' creative imagination.

As well as musicians there were jugglers, dancing bear trainers, and buffoons of every kind. Here and there professional dancing girls make their appearance, and, from what we can deduce from the records, seem to have indulged in the most remarkable contortions to tickle the jaded fancy of a king or lickerous lord.

*   *   *

73
Various entertainments:
(a) Wrestling.
(b) Bear-baiting.
(c) A performing bear.
(d) A woman acrobat
balancing on the tips of swords,
with musical accompaniment.

74
The spade and the distaff.

Among the regular travellers on the ill-kept roads of the time were messengers of many kinds. Inhabitants of a remote fortress must have waited far more eagerly than we do for the postman to arrive. There were no regular deliveries. Royal messengers carried royal commands, title deeds, summonses and other communications about the country as and when the need arose. Certain confidential letters were entrusted to secret emissaries in England and abroad; and even today there is a lingering romantic air about the designation of Queen's Messenger.

Letters from the monarch or from a lord were rarely written in the sender's own hand. He would dictate to a scribe, usually his chaplain or the chaplain's clerk, who would transfer the message to parchment, to be sealed with the royal or baronial signet and then despatched. The carrier of good tidings could usually rely on receiving a suitable gift when he reached the addressee – a practice long fallen into disuse, and presenting far too many complications to the modern postal service. On the other hand, the modern postman runs little risk, as a bearer of bad news, of being executed, losing his tongue, or being made to swallow the parchment on which the offending missive was written.

Some messengers did indeed have to carry some pretty unpleasant packages. The king frequently ordered one of his trusted men to take the butchered remains of a treasonable criminal to be impaled on spikes or otherwise displayed as a moral lesson to folk elsewhere in the realm. Edward III paid

> Sir William de Faryngton, knight, for the costs and expenses he had incurred for transporting the four quarters of the body of Sir John of Mistreworth, knight, to different parts of England.

75
Delivery of a sealed missive.

One doubts whether the towns chosen as recipients of these grisly souvenirs would be all that pleased with the arrival of the royal mail.

In a society bound by so many feudal and manorial regulations as to be virtually static, opportunities for 'free enterprise' might seem to have been non-existent. Yet no society, however totalitarian, however inhibited by kings, dictators, bureaucrats or churchmen it may appear, has ever been utterly stagnant. If the human race can be relied on at any stage of history and under any circumstances to produce one type of person, that will be the smart operator, the bender of rules: the fast talker, the pouncer on elusive opportunity, living on into our own time as the smart alec, the wide boy, the wheeler-dealer.

Among these in medieval days was a man who often acquired his wares by fraud, theft and other dubious transactions, who probably sold at inflated prices whenever and wherever he found a gullible purchaser, especially at town or country fairs and markets, who was condemned as a vagabond in many official edicts, yet whose absence would sorely have incommoded the country dweller. This was the pedlar, bringing to village and hamlet the things which would otherwise never have been seen there. Village shops were unknown. The nearest town was as a rule not near enough for the cottager to reach. 'A day's shopping' in a busy High Street was a notion not yet conceived.

The only provider of hats, ribbons, gloves, domestic pots and gewgaws was the pedlar, who knew his markets and had the right patter for each of them, large and small. The cheapjack of his day, he brought improbable bargains to the naïve, and amusement to all. He was not too reluctant to consider barter rather than cash transactions: from one place he might take home-made napery to trade for goose quills, from another beeswax in exchange for a strip of fur or hide, a sack of salt for a length of cloth. Impertinently direct approach to the lord's castle invited a snub; but the ladies of the household were not above sending a serving wench down to the village to indulge in a few fancies, and a chapman who could guarantee regular supplies of some cherished commodity to the steward was likely to build up a good reputation for himself and make it possible, eventually, to cease travelling and set up a sort of wholesale distribution centre. A pedlar could become a merchant, using his old contacts to supply or draw from his warehouse, and commissioning others to set off with their packs along the highways and by-ways of the land. Even then he was rarely regarded as a respectable tradesman: the country's economy and all its social structure still rested on the earth, and people who lived a perambulatory life, buying and selling, were instinctively dubbed rogues and vagabonds, no matter how much one desired their wares.

That charlatans trod the roads and paths there can be no doubt. As well as the persuasive vendor of shoddy goods, the disguised outlaws and the sneak thieves and pickpockets – as common at tournaments and country markets as at markets and race meetings today – there were many who travelled under the respectable cloak of healers dedicated to alleviating ills of the body or, even more acute, those of the soul.

Some kings and lords employed their own physicians, bound to them by indentures, in return paying a comfortable salary and granting many privileges and exemptions. Some of these had studied medicine as far as they were able, or as far as they were allowed: the Church was the governor of all education, and the Church did not approve of medical studies, its generously endowed and selflessly run hospitals being mainly places of prayer and rest. The dividing line between the apothecary and the alchemist – and all too often between superstition and science – was a fine one; and surgery, without anaesthetics or antiseptics, was a butchery which few survived.

On those who could not afford even the doubtful skills of a resident physician, the travelling quack exercised a fearful influence. He and the local wise woman, rivals in the same field, offered concoctions of drugs and herbs privately or in the market-place, in each case announcing each brew as the ultimate, universal panacea. There were ointments to soothe, to cure skin and bone complaints, and such treatments as a compress of boiled beetles and crickets to cure 'the stone'. Violent purges were much recommended, as was blood-letting, either by opening a vein and controlling the flow with a sort of adjustable tourniquet, or by application of leeches to bloat themselves on the blood. A twelfth-century manuscript praises the virtues of this treatment, which

> makes the mind sincere, purges the brain, reforms the bladder, warms the marrow, opens the hearing, checks tears, removes nausea, benefits the stomach, invites digestion, evokes the voice, builds up the sense, moves the bowels, enriches sleep, removes anxiety, nourishes good health.

Churchmen, however, insisted that all ailments were divine punishment for sin or, at best, a loving discipline which must be borne with courage and humility. St Bernard, founder of the Cistercian order, forbade his monks to study medicine, to take medicine, or to consult a doctor. Yet it was allowed that some holy relics and holy places might, by the grace of God, have a healing influence. St Winifred's Well at Holywell in North Wales was, and by some still is, credited with miraculous properties for curing nervous disorders. Lady's Well, near Woolpit in Suffolk, is a spring whose waters were held from the twelfth century onwards to work wonders on diseases of the eye, and its revenue from pilgrims was so considerable that the great abbot Samson of Bury St Edmunds went personally to Rome to secure the monopoly. The halt and the blind, the sick and wounded, all made their way to the shrines of saints such as Edmund and Thomas à Becket, for whose murder Henry II was forced to do such humiliating

76
(left) An emergency operation without anaesthetics.
(right) Morning surgery.

penance, or sought holy relics to touch in the hope of cure. In Chaucer's *Canterbury Tales* are assembled a number of such pilgrims, sincere and otherwise, each with his own story to tell and each adding a facet to a vivid picture of the medieval world in which they lived, together with its contemporary beliefs and obsessions.

When the Black Death harrowed the country in the middle of the fourteenth century, doctors and quacks and clerics of all kinds and persuasions sought a multitude of remedies. It was said that newly baked bread applied warm to the lips would soak up the poison. Fires were made to smoke abundantly in order to purify the air; or for that same purpose, strange as it sounds, animals such as goats were brought into a sufferer's room.

Again the official verdict was that this was a visitation brought on by human wickedness. Repentance was the only answer.

Even sin had its antidote, however, according to another group of itinerant dealers.

*　　*　　*

The pardoner in the *Canterbury Tales* is a greedy, sly rogue and no good advertisement for his calling. Chaucer was not the only one to condemn the activities of such hypocrites, trading on the superstitions and fears of their more gullible fellows by offering indulgences guaranteed to absolve the purchaser from any number of penances and pains in this life and the next. Originally the purpose of an indulgence was to shorten time spent in Purgatory or in fulfilling the terms of a punishment laid down in this

world. To obtain one, the supplicant must make a donation to help the Church in its work. A nobleman who had, willingly or by some religious dictate, committed himself to, say, a long period of fasting or chastisement, or promised to make an arduous pilgrimage, could release himself by buying an indulgence from a travelling pardoner. The poor would pay more often in kind than in cash. In certain circumstances the Pope himself would grant a plenary indulgence – a blanket forgiveness, such as Urban II's promise of remission to all who volunteered to join the first Crusade and liberate Jerusalem. He also issued papers to authorised pardoners who sent all the payments collected to Rome. But far more common were the forgeries touted around by 'con men' who pocketed the takings for themselves. Many added a touch of apparent authenticity by showing to their awed customers the relics of saints which they carried about with them, supposedly brought back from pilgrimage: Chaucer's pardoner, for instance, claimed to have a shred of sail from St Peter's boat.

There were other men of religion trudging about the country on foot – barefoot, if they were strict observers of the rules of their order. Mendicant friars were enjoined to live and work among the poor and accept that poverty for themselves. They must eat only food which was freely offered, and never take money. They brought comfort to the sick and bereaved, and in many cases were capable of preaching finer sermons than the illiterate village priest and of answering doctrinal questions which worried the frightened peasant. This did not always commend them to the parish incumbent, especially when they began to interpret the rules of chastity and poverty to suit their own inclinations, looking for richer food and accommodation, accepting money readily, and so appropriating offerings which the resident priest felt belonged to him. They visited the lord in his castle and dined well at his table, flattering him with learned discourse and tolerantly hearing the confession of himself and his lady. It was this lax and self-indulgent species of friar who aroused the scorn of more austere reformers such as Wyclif and his followers.

Roaming preachers of independent views were approved of neither by the Church nor officialdom, since many of their views on Christian charity and austerity could all too easily take on a sharp edge which the common people might be tempted to turn against their well-to-do lords and prelates. On their lips a religious sermon could become a political harangue. Attempts were made to silence them, often by throwing them into prison. John Ball, one of the fieriest of itinerant preachers of democracy, was in fact in jail when Wat Tyler's Kentish rebellion broke out and had to be released by the peasants as they marched on London. His message was heard more often out of doors than in the castle hall or chapel:

> If God had willed that there should be serfs he would have said at the beginning of the world who should be serf and who should be lord.

Perhaps we cannot number such folk among welcome visitors. They may have evoked a response in the village but could scarcely have expected a hearty greeting at the gates of castle or manor house. The occupants of such establishments were doubtless delighted when, the Kentish uprising having failed, John Ball was hanged, drawn and quartered, and the pieces taken by royal messenger from one place to another as a bloody warning of what awaited any other would-be agitators.

CHAPTER VI

FROM FORTRESS TO MANOR HOUSE

We owe our familiar colourful picture of castles as the turreted white palaces of chivalry, with knights errant riding forth to the rescue of fair damsels or jousting for their favours, largely to Edward I and his grandson Edward III. Worried by a falling off in the number of young men coming forward for knighthood, and the growing tendency to commute military service into scutage, Edward I tried to lure them with ceremonial and pageantry. He held 'Round Table' conclaves, re-interpreted Arthurian legend, and no longer frowned, as some of his predecessors had done, on tournaments.

Personal combat in the castle lists could be exciting and risky, but rarely resulted in anything worse than broken limbs. Tournaments caused far bloodier casualties, being in effect miniature battles. Competing lords drew up their followers in battle array and, in the absence of a real war, practised the martial arts in what might start as a friendly match but could, in the heat of the moment, turn into a real rough-house. There were often rich rewards: contestants would gamble away such property as they had, sometimes returning penniless from the field of combat or the lists.

The Church had always frowned on these exhibitions. One Pope decreed that men killed in tourney were not entitled to Christian burial. Another specifically outlawed tournaments and appealed to young men who wished to practise combat to do so on Crusade in the Holy Land. Various kings, too, were unhappy about the violence and the possible loss of needed fighting men. They rarely intervened, however, when a contest was being organised by powerful barons: instead, they solved the matter in their usual way by demanding a fee for the royal permission to go ahead.

Edward III went several steps further in the encouragement of chivalry, building up a picturesque, mannered court life which tempted the young and ambitious to enter this fashionable world, or at the very least spurred them to emulate its formalities in their own circle. At a reception in 1344 he is said to have picked up the countess of Salisbury's garter when it fell and, in reproof of his courtiers' meaning grins, fastened it to his own leg and said, 'Honi soit qui mal y pense' (Shamed be he who thinks evil of it), which was to become the motto of the Order of the Garter and be incorporated in

77
Edward III in the regalia of the Order of the Garter.

the royal coat of arms. The Garter was created by Edward as an order of chivalry for himself, his children, and a few chosen knights. To house its ideals worthily he put in hand a massive rebuilding programme at Windsor castle, so intensive that

> almost all the masons and carpenters throughout the whole of England were brought to that building, so that hardly anyone could have any good mason or carpenter, except in secret, on account of the king's prohibition.

Edward, like his grandfather, was under the spell of the Round Table stories and wished to re-create something like Arthur's legendary court at Windsor. It was not, however, until after his death that work began on St George's chapel, in which the annual Garter ceremony is held on St George's Day. Membership of the order still lies exclusively in the gift of the sovereign.

However sincerely he might strive for the revival of a courtly way of life which in any case owed more to myth than history, Edward III was confronted by harsh realities working against his ideals. His claims to the French throne plunged the country again and again into strife, and led ultimately to the Hundred Years' War. The bubonic plague known as the Black Death killed an estimated third of the population between 1348 and 1350, and returned at intervals up to 1369 to take further toll. One effect was to put the surviving peasants in a strong position to shake off many feudal restrictions and bargain with their landlords for wages and better conditions of employment. Another was the loss of knights, both through this plague and through the recurrent wars, seriously weakening the royal levies. In addition, the increasing expense of horses, armour, fees and subsequent upkeep of one's accoutrements and prestige made many of those entitled to train for the knighthood reluctant to go through the ritual. A young man eager for glory but possessing no land might sell his services to a lord who preferred to stay at home, pay scutage, and cultivate his estates. Some with no intention of ever riding into battle would acquire land on the usual terms of knight service, and at once commute this service into cash payment. Hence many a squire remained a squire, until the word gradually assumed the meaning which has lasted to this day.

The king and those barons due to supply him with knight service found it increasingly necessary to hire mercenaries, largely from Wales and northern Europe. These hirelings might swear allegiance to one lord only, but they were not under the old restrictions of service, and frequently changed masters in return for more pay and more comforts. Castles in which they served have been referred to as castles of 'livery and maintenance': the soldiers of fortune adopted, if only temporarily, the heraldic badges of their employers on their uniform or livery, in return for maintenance.

When lodged in such a castle, these men could not but be regarded as strangers in the midst of the family and its long-established household. Their alien presence had two effects on castle building, apparent in Edward I's reign and even more marked by the time of Edward III and Richard II.

In the first place, soldiers who supported a baron only for money, maintenance and the promise of loot had little intrinsic loyalty, nor were they bound to him by any fief. Offered better conditions elsewhere, they might simply walk out – or turn on him. For safety's sake it was best not to mix too freely with the mercenaries but to keep their quarters distinct from

78
A 15th-century, cosy private room with glazed and leaded window and a fireplace – a great change from the open hearth, open slits, and draughty hall of earlier centuries.

those of the family. Many a lord or his constable shut himself and his more trusted retainers away in a gatehouse so that in time of mutiny they could command the entrance. This led to a reversion to the principle of the keep: strong towers reminiscent of earlier days can be found at Nunney in Somerset, and on top of the motte at Warkworth in Northumberland.

In the second place, since the old comradely pleasures of the great hall could not with any great enjoyment be shared with the mercenaries, the tendency of the lord and his family to withdraw into private chambers was intensified. At the same time greater emphasis was laid on creature comforts. Since one was not merely to sleep but to spend a large part of one's private life in rooms set apart, these rooms needed more amenities. Chimneys replaced draughty open windows or crude flues, and glass became increasingly common in the windows themselves. Washbasins were inset in the walls, discharging dirty water through pipes and gargoyles on the outside of the building. The 'withdrawing' room was on its way to becoming the drawing room. The communal hall would eventually become the servants' hall or be reduced to a mere passage linking a number of smaller rooms – the entrance 'hall' of any private house in our own time.

A castle embodying both aspects mentioned above is that at Bodiam on the Kent-Sussex border. It was in 1385 that Sir Edward Dalyngruge was granted the licence to build himself a fortification 'in defence of the adjacent country against the king's enemies'. Standing some miles inland beside what is now a tranquil stretch of the river Rother, Bodiam was then within the danger zone of French raids on the Kent and Sussex coast and on villages behind the Cinque Ports. Dalyngruge himself had good reason to fear French vengeance. In partnership with the unscrupulous Edward Knollys he had rampaged through France as a bandit rather than a soldier, plundering and holding widows and young women of good family to ransom. Returning with enough plunder to build himself a castle, he married an heiress whose property included the land at Bodiam.

The castle has two quite distinct ranges of rooms, one for the master and the other for his retainers. After such a career as a blackguard, Sir Edward probably trusted no one and was shielding himself not just from a foreign enemy but from possible unrest in the ranks of his own hirelings. But in addition, although the defensive moat and splendid towers present the appearance of a formidable stronghold, the emphasis of the interior is much more on domesticity than in most such buildings, and it was in fact well on its way to reaching the standards of a comfortable manor house.

There is a third interesting feature at Bodiam, of great significance in castle building or adaptation from now on. In its gatehouse are not merely arrow slits but gun ports.

It has often been said that the introduction of gunpowder and cannons into warfare sounded the death knell of the castle. This is highly questionable. The earliest bombards and other such weapons could not compete in destructive power against a wall of solid masonry with that of a heavy siege engine, the propellant force of the gunpowder was kept low for fear of bursting the barrel – which nevertheless often blew up in the gunner's face – and they could fire little more formidable than bolts and improvised grapeshot. Though probably used in the field by Edward I against the Scots, cannon only gradually became a major weapon of war.

79
Bodiam, Sussex.

But it nevertheless became necessary for defenders as well as attackers to have cannon, and in addition to the provision of gun platforms and ports in all new fortifications, arrow slits in existing buildings were opened out by means of a round aperture to hold the gun, producing the appearance of a keyhole. In his lavish additions to Kenilworth, John of Gaunt included two towers capable of holding cannon if needed.

There were, though, not many new fortresses. War had grown more mobile, and dogged sieges were out of fashion. A few castles still played an important part in the Wars of the Roses. In 1480, towards their end, Lord Hastings began to build one at Kirby Muxloe in Leicestershire whose comforts would be worthy of his high rank as Edward IV's Grand Chamberlain and whose strength would protect him against the warring factions. His castle, too, had gun ports, but they were of little avail to Hastings, who did not live to see the building completed: Richard III had him executed in 1483. Henry VII's policy of impoverishing his nobles and putting an end to internal strife, together with the great strides being made in commerce and so the rise in importance of merchants, civilian magnates and tradesmen of all kinds, meant a swing towards smaller, cosier residences – at most, in extreme cases, a fortified manor house rather than a stone citadel. Fearing a French invasion, Henry VIII built or reinforced several coastal castles, but these incorporated few residential amenities for king or baron: they were basically huge gun turrets.

By the time of the Civil War, ordnance was powerful enough to smash its way into such castles as tried to hold out in the traditional way: looking once more at Arundel, we find it first surrendering to the Royalists and then being besieged by the Parliamentarians who, firing from vantage points such as the church tower, made it unsafe for the defenders to move about and then, to bring them to their knees, carried out the classic move of diverting the water supply so that the castle well ran dry.

Few castles were utterly destroyed. The strength of the walls was usually such that demolition would cost more than the resulting material was worth, though in several cases Cromwell's men did their worst. Even by the eighteenth century a contractor found the flint and lime construction of Bungay's remaining walls so sturdy that he was unable to break them up, as planned, to sell the stones off for road-mending. When however, it was considered advisable to render a castle useless for military purposes it could be 'slighted': that is, important sections of the curtain walls would be breached, roofs stripped off to let the elements do their work on the interior, and towers mined and enfeebled. Some suffered greater damage than others: Corfe castle was reduced to a fanged ruin; the main contours of Caerphilly are still in fairly good repair, its slighting symbolised by a cracked, leaning round tower.

With improvements in national administration and communications, and with royal domestic life and royal functionaries concentrated in

London, the king no longer needed to be forever travelling and so needed fewer of his own castles. This was just as well, since a chronic lack of royal funds meant that many were falling of their own accord into disrepair. The barons also, by the late fourteenth and early fifteenth centuries, were quitting or refashioning the last of their historic strongholds.

*   *   *

Even in unsettled times some lords had preferred to build comfortable granges for themselves, sometimes raising timbered residential halls within the castle baileys, or choosing a site overlooking one of their manorial villages. The castle, left in charge of a constable, was there for emergencies only. Such separate manors might at first copy the layout of the familiar castle, even to the extent of having a large hall as the focus of the household, and might be lightly fortified and continue to be called castles; but gradually the towers and crenellations became ornamental rather than practical.

80
Stokesay castle, Shropshire. The central great hall is flanked by the original tower, topped in the 16th century with timber and plaster, and a 13th-century tower built by the Ludlows.

At Stokesay in Shropshire is an example of an interesting sequence wherein an unfortified hall was strengthened in the thirteenth century by a stone tower and the addition of a curtain wall; another hall – the one which

The stair to the solar at the end of the great hall, Stokesay.

we can see today – was built early in the following century; and then in the sixteenth century a half-timbered gatehouse was added, delightful to study but of no defensive importance. All in all it makes an identifiable progress from residential hall to fortified manor and then to a purely residential house once more.

Tattershall in Lincolnshire offers what at first glance seems to be the tall keep remaining from some old fortress, but closer inspection reveals it as a private house fashioned in the likeness of a great tower. There had been a small castle here in the thirteenth century, two of whose towers stood to either side of the new work planned in 1434 by Ralph Cromwell, Henry VI's Lord Treasurer. His great hall of residence has vanished, as so many timber halls did, and one might be tempted to assume that in its day it provided living quarters while the keep provided refuge. The keep itself, however, was also purely residential: its windows too large for a defensive tower, and its finely vaulted interior lovingly embellished by first-rate craftsmen. Over 300,000 red bricks were used for the body of the building, probably imported from the Continent, with several thousand smaller ones specially made for parapets and other features. A story of some suspense attaches to four of the interior splendours. The chimney-pieces of Ancaster limestone, carved with heraldic devices and one with the Treasurer's Purse in its spandrel, were almost lost to the nation at the beginning of this century. With the tower derelict and falling apart inside, the chimney-pieces were removed for sale to an American buyer. Lord Curzon, to whose beneficence we also owe the preservation of Bodiam, rushed a bill through

82
Tattershall, Lincolnshire.

Parliament to forbid their export, and had a watch set on the ports so that they should not be smuggled out. It took three months to track them down, after which they were returned to their rightful home.

At about the time Tattershall was being finished in 1448 work started on another brick castle, or so-called castle, at Herstmonceux. This, again, was more of a castellated mansion. Sir Roger Fiennes, also a Treasurer – Henry VI's Treasurer of the Household – still required royal permission to crenellate, but when he got to work his battlements were installed for show and not for defence. The relatively thin brick walls, graceful gatehouse towers and slender bastions would not have stood up to heavy siege machinery or even to early cannon. The workmen were almost certainly Flemish and, unlike the brick-makers for Tattershall, worked on the spot, digging clay from the surrounding land and in the process making the moat which still prettily girdles the castle. The pink reflections of those walls in

83
One of the Tattershall fireplaces.

84
The gatehouse of Herstmonceux castle, Sussex, built by Henry VI's Treasurer, Sir Roger de Fiennes, well-nigh dismantled by the eccentric second wife of Canon Hare of Winchester, sold by another eccentric inheritor, and at one stage left to apparent decay until restored and ultimately taken over by the Royal Greenwich Observatory.

the water make Herstmonceux, indeed, pretty rather than challenging. Inside were echoes of this elegance: suites of well-proportioned rooms, private staircases and spacious corridors, making it comparatively simple for a Restoration inheritor of the property to introduce stylish stucco ceilings and 'a great deal of fine carving' by Grinling Gibbons. Its twentieth-century function is that of headquarters for the Royal Greenwich Observatory staff.

As the late medieval and Tudor magnates and aspiring gentry adopted the terms 'house', 'manor' or 'hall' for their sumptuous edifices – Wingfield, Hatfield, Little Moreton, Haddon, Burghley and so many others – and explored the possibilities of brick, tile and half-timbering, the stone castles were gradually abandoned. The fate of the castle at Lewes, property of the proud de Warenne family, typifies that of many.

After the Norman Conquest, William de Warenne was presented with the Rape of Lewes and started to fortify a site above the Sussex Ouse with the usual motte-and-bailey pattern, though with one unusual feature: it was not uncommon to have a motte and two baileys, but Lewes set out with two mottes, man-made but so strong that on one of them it was possible to set the later flint keep. Towers were built on to this keep in the thirteenth century, and in the early fourteenth the main walls were strengthened and an outer barbican added beyond the moat to reinforce the gatehouse, incorporating two drawbridges. With his wife Gundrada, daughter of the Conqueror, de Warenne introduced the Cluniac fraternity to England with the establishment of St Pancras' priory at Lewes. He died in Lewes castle in

1088 from wounds received during the siege of Pevensey, and his son then endowed a priory at Castle Acre in Norfolk as a limb of St Pancras.

The last Warenne died in 1347 and was buried in Lewes priory, to be succeeded by one of the Fitzalan earls of Arundel who did not use Lewes as even a satellite residence but allowed it to decay. By the end of the century the castle had been ransacked by the townsfolk and left derelict. In 1620 much of the remaining fabric was sold off in loads of flint and freestone, though the more substantial parts stood firm: by the following century the barbican and keep were being used for storage by a local wool merchant, who took up residence in the barbican and fitted up the keep as a summerhouse. What remained by 1850 was saved by the Sussex Archaeological Society, who began renting it as a museum and now have their offices and records there.

The family fortress at Castle Acre, built within earthworks dating from Roman times, was similarly abandoned after 1347. Its keep has disappeared, the remains of the moat are half choked with overgrown masonry, and the only tangible souvenirs are courses of old stone incorporated in some of the houses, and one rubble and stone gateway with two drum towers standing athwart the aptly named Bailey Street. The core of the present village delineates a ghost, as it were, of the old bailey wall.

Another relic of the immediate post-Conquest years, Belvoir castle, went through a number of transformations. Built by William the Conqueror's standard-bearer, it had crumbled to ruin by the sixteenth century and then restored in a succession of different forms by the dukes of Rutland. Finally, in the early nineteenth century, it was equipped once more with turrets and

85
The hall of Sutton Courtenay manor house, Berkshire, largely of 15th-century origin, in a village which still retains its Norman hall and the remains of a 14th-century abbey.

86
Boothby Pagnell, a Norman manor house near Grantham in Lincolnshire.

both a square tower and a round one, crenellated into a sham Gothic fantasy which stands to this day.

Some ruins were put to worthy use. Bricks and stone from the duke of Bedford's derelict Fulbrook castle, near Warwick, were taken by Sir William Compton at the end of the fifteenth century to help in the construction of his house near the deserted village of Compton Superior. The location he chose was known originally as Compton-in-the-Hole, but this was later changed to Compton Wynyates, meaning 'windy vale'. Its banqueting hall and minstrels' gallery are in the tradition of the early medieval hall; but the whole atmosphere is Tudor, with its inner richness and outer brickwork, topped by twisting Tudor chimneys.

As we have noted, the Black Death altered the balance between feudal or manorial lord and enslaved peasant. Labourers in the fields began to demand as rights what they had hitherto hardly dared plead for as favours. When rebellious spirits demanded extortionate wages or withheld their labour and contented themselves with cultivating their own patches, laws were passed to stabilise wages and obligations. They caused further disintegration. Mass outbreaks such as the Peasants' Revolt under the combined leadership of Wat Tyler, John Ball and Jack Straw, and later Jack Cade's Rebellion, were ferociously suppressed; but there was no going back to the days of absolute serfdom. Men who did not choose to work on the land found fresh opportunities of employment and advancement in the burgeoning towns and cities, and quite early on some boroughs offered the inducement that any serf who ran away from his master and managed to sustain himself in a charter town for a year and a day without being recaptured was thereafter a free man.

The towns were taking over from the fields. Even the descendants of the great magnates began to devote as much time to urban interests as to their fragmented estates. Lesser knights and the squirearchy played a vigorous part in exploiting the new commercial opportunities. Lords invested their rents in the wool trade or in import businesses, and used their family influence to have relatives and sycophants appointed to key posts in town, city and seaport. Land deals, property deals and commercial speculation became of paramount importance. Even during the Wars of the Roses, the small bodies of fighting men involved did slight damage to the countryside or the everyday life of the townsman, compared with conflicts in previous centuries, and business suffered hardly at all. When it did, there was an outcry. General indignation at the mishandling of relations with the Continental staple towns, with the Hanseatic League and Denmark, had more to do with the outbreak of those wars and public opinion on them than any partisanship for Yorkist or Lancastrian.

So the castle lost its arrogance, the manor lost its automatic rights to labour and specified taxes; land was partitioned and sold off, the magnates went into trade, the descendants of one-time villeins leased and farmed

87
The barbican, Lewes castle.

their own acres. Some village craftsmen undoubtedly suffered. Without the security of the manorial workshops' full-time demand for their services, they found themselves often in competition with the better organised industries of the town, and either moved into such a town or doggedly worked out complicated agreements with their neighbours and folk in neighbouring villages.

Where a town had itself had a castle, that too dwindled in importance. Many were abandoned or used – as at Norwich – for city or county jails. Some, in later centuries, became museums. Today our first impulse, on seeing a noble pile in the distance, is to check in our guidebook whether it is cared for on our behalf by the National Trust or the Department of the Environment or whether some gallant family is still trying to preserve it

88
Wingfield, Suffolk: the 14th-century wall and gatehouse of a moated castle, complete with drawbridge, embrace a Tudor house in a rural setting from which war and baronial conflicts seem far away in time and space.

with the aid of conducted tours, teas, collections of ancient motor cars in the stables, or zoos and aviaries in the demesne.

Thornbury in Gloucestershire would seem to have been the last building project in England to be described categorically as a castle. Conceived by Edward Stafford, duke of Buckingham, it began to take shape in 1511 but came to a halt when Henry VIII ordered his beheading in 1521. Its long west front and tower remain impressive, but the battlements and arrow slits are unashamedly ornamental, the bay windows are too spacious for a defensive building, and the whole thing is crowned by remarkable triple groupings of convoluted brick chimneys, like fantastic watch-towers yet utterly unmilitary in character.

The horrors of disease, deprivation and torture, of starvation during sieges and of death in foul dungeons, recede into the background when we contemplate the romantic silhouette of some old tower and battlements on the skyline. Romance survives; everyday reality conveniently fades. Edward Gibbon was right:

There is more pleasure in building castles in the air than on the ground.

Select Bibliography

BENNETT, H.S. *Life on the English Manor* (Cambridge University Press, 1974)

BRAYLEY, E.W. *Ancient Castles of England and Wales* (Longman, Hurst, 1825)

BROWN, R.A. *English Medieval Castles* (Batsford, 1954)

FRY, P.S. *Medieval Castles* (David & Charles, 1975)

GIES, J. & F. *Life in a Medieval Castle* (Abelard-Schuman, 1975)

HART, ROGER *English Life in Chaucer's Day* (Wayland, 1973)

JUSSERAND, J.J. *English Wayfaring Life in the Middle Ages* (Benn, 1889; Methuen, 1961)

KOTKER, NORMAN (ed) *The Horizon Book of the Middle Ages* (Cassell, 1969)

LINCOLN, E.F. *The Medieval Legacy* (MacGibbon & Kee, 1961)

MITCHELL, R.J., & LEYS, M.D.R. *A History of the English People* (Longmans, Green, 1950; Pan, 1967)

MYERS, A.R. *England in the Late Middle Ages* (Penguin, 1952)

O'NEIL, B.H.St.J. *Castles* (HMSO, 1973)

STENTON, D.M. *English Society in the Early Middle Ages* (Penguin, 1952)

Index